Discovering
the
Mystery
of
Jesus
Christ

K. R. HERUM

All rights reserved. This book is protected by the copyright laws of the United States of America. This book may not be copied or reprinted for commercial gain or profit. The use of short quotations or occasional page copying for personal or group study is permitted and encouraged.

Unless designated, all Scripture is taken from the New American Standard Bible. Copyright © 1960, 1962, 1963, 1968, 1971, 1972, 1973, 1975, 1977, 1995 by The Lockman Foundation, La Habra, Calif. All rights reserved.

Emphasis within Scripture is the authors own.

Self-Published
1st Edition © 2013
2st Edition © 2025

All rights reserved

© Copyright 2013 – K. R. Herum
All rights reserved

Library of Congress Catalog Card Number: 1-961980981

ISBN-13:978-0615848617
ISBN-10:0615848613

*I am grateful to my parents,
who raised me to know and love Jesus,
which is the foundation from which I write.
I am so thankful and love you both.*

TABLE OF CONTENTS

Introduction		Page
Chapter 1	Called by God	1
Chapter 2	Chosen by God	15
Chapter 3	Going Your Own Way	27
Chapter 4	The Life of Jesus	41
Chapter 5	The Mystery of Christ Jesus	67
Chapter 6	The Name above All Names	81
Chapter 7	Going Jesus' Way	101
Chapter 8	The Exchanged Life	115
Chapter 9	Life in the Holy Spirit	131
Chapter 10	The Kingdom Life	149
Chapter 11	Relationship with Jesus	165
Chapter 12	Grace and Glory	187
Appendix		211

INTRODUCTION

I have written this book for those of you who are truly seeking to find more of God regardless if you don't know much about Him or if you have been in church your whole life. This book gives you an easy-to-read synopsis of the essential information from the Bible that is necessary to understand who Jesus is, why He came to earth, and what He wants from you in order for you to make an informed decision whether to follow Him. My hope is that through reading this book, you will fall in love with Jesus, enjoy a life of peace and joy with God, and spend eternity with Him.

The first half of this book explains how God made it possible through Jesus Christ for each of us to have a personal relationship with Him and what we must do to receive that relationship. The second half of this book will then seek to explain the many dynamics and awesome blessings that come with being in relationship with Jesus, as well as the cost of following Him.

This book is really a Bible study. I intentionally tried to include every key verse on the topics I wrote about so that those of you who really want to study and understand what the Bible says on a given topic will have all possible verses at your fingertips. The Bible verses are really part of the text and would be best read as such. Verses of Scripture are the true word from God that have the same power as His spoken word on the day of creation when God said "let there be..." and it was. May God give revelation as you study who Jesus Christ is and the abundant life He is offering you.

The Bible says that "now is the day of salvation, now is the day of His favor." "Today, if you hear His voice calling you, do not harden your heart" (see Hebrews 3:15). Do not be slow to respond to God; do not miss your chance, for Jesus Christ is coming back soon.

> "For He says, 'In a favorable time I listened to you, and in a day of salvation I have helped you.' **Behold, now is the favorable time; behold, now is the day of salvation**" (2 Corinthians 6:2).

CHAPTER 1

Called by God

You may not have noticed but God has been speaking to you your whole life. Let me suggest a few ways God has been calling you and trying to communicate His thoughts to you in the hope that you can look back and realize, "Yeah, God has been trying to get my attention, I just wasn't listening!"

Nature

God has left us a testimony of Himself in nature all around us. "The heavens declare the glory of God and the sky above proclaims His handiwork" (Psalm 19:1). The splendor, majesty, and beauty of mountains, the peaceful meadows full of flowers, the towering trees of the forests, and the power of the waves crashing on the beach all declare His handiwork. The sky, thunder and lighting, outer space planets and solar systems all testify of a God bigger than we are! Science reveals over and over again that our world has been awesomely and magnificently made. Nature reveals a lot about its Maker and leaves us no excuse for not knowing Him.

"For the wrath of God is revealed from heaven against all ungodliness and unrighteousness of men who suppress the truth in unrighteousness, because that which is known about God is evident within them; for God made it evident to them. **For since the creation of the world His invisible attributes, His eternal power and divine nature, have been clearly seen, being understood through what has been made**, so that they are without excuse" (Romans 1:18-20).

Miracles

Not only do the glorious laws of nature testify that there is a God of order and design but so do the supernatural "exceptions" that break into reality; the modern-day miracles that we have all experienced at least once, if not more often in our lives. Most of us have experienced God healing our bodies or saving our life from danger when there is no explanation except God! There are also the dreams or visions, and the times we thought we heard God's voice—and we probably did. There are even people on the earth today to whom Jesus has personally appeared.

Testimonies, Stories, Media

There is also the witness of believers you know who have told you about their experiences with God. History has millions of testimonies of what God has done in people's lives through the ages. Today God is still speaking through books, movies, and music. One example is the multitude of apocalyptic movies warning us that the world will not go on indefinitely. God is constantly speaking!

Jesus' Life on Earth

The greatest way God has spoken to us and revealed Himself to us is in Jesus Christ. When Jesus Christ became flesh and walked on the earth, He was the image of the invisible God. He radiated God's glory and was the exact representation of God's nature because the fullness of God's deity dwelled in his human body.

> "**He is the image of the invisible God**, the firstborn of all creation" (Colossians 1:15).

> "For **in him the whole fullness of deity dwells bodily**" (Colossians 2:9).

> "In these last days **he [*God*] has spoken to us by his Son**, whom he appointed the heir of all things, through whom also he created the world. **He [*Jesus*] is the radiance of the glory of God** and the exact imprint of his nature" (Hebrews 1:2-3).

Jesus was the Word of God, telling us about the Father and revealing His glory to us by becoming flesh and dwelling among us (see John 1:1, 14). Jesus Himself claimed that He was the only way to God the Father in heaven, and that to know Jesus is to know the Father.

"I am the way, and the truth, and the life. **No one comes to the Father except through me. If you had known me, you would have known my Father also.** From now on you do know him and have seen him" (John 14:6-7).

The Bible

Today we have the written record of Jesus' life that reveals God the Father to us in the Bible. The whole Bible is God's written word to us, not man's word.

"No prophecy of Scripture comes from someone's own interpretation. For no prophecy was ever produced by the will of man, but **men spoke from God as they were carried along by the Holy Spirit**" (2 Peter 1:20-21).

"**All Scripture is breathed out by God** and profitable for teaching, for reproof, for correction, and for training in righteousness, that the man of God may be competent, equipped for every good work" (2 Timothy 3:16-17).

If we read the Bible with an open mind, God will reveal Himself to us. The reason I quote so much Scripture in this book is that I believe the written word of God in the Bible has the power to speak to your heart, change your thinking, and transform your life. I am not worried about the doubts that the skeptics of our day have voiced. I know that the word of God by itself is living, active, and powerful enough to defend itself (see Hebrews 4:12). Jesus once said to the skeptics in His midst, "If anyone's will is to do God's will, he will know whether the teaching is from God or whether I am speaking on my own authority" (John 7:17). I believe the same is true for you. If there is a place deep in your heart that is seeking truth and you are willing to receive what is true, God will reveal Himself to you and you will know the truth, and the truth will set you free (John 8:32).

Still Quite Voice Deep Inside

Another way God speaks to us is through the still quiet voice deep down inside of us. Somehow there is a "knowing in our knower" that there is something bigger than ourselves. Somehow, we know we were made for something special. For years, I have struggled with what I call the "Walter Mitty complex." *The Secret*

Life of Walter Mitty is a short story written in 1939 by James Thurber that was released as a movie in 2013. It's about an ordinary guy who lives life vicariously through daydreams, fantasizing about his own greatness while working a mundane job. Somehow, deep down inside, we all know that we were created for something bigger than the mundane, and that there is a God with a bigger plan for us, who has a destiny we haven't yet discovered or fulfilled. The hunger and dissatisfaction that we so often feel testifies to it. The feeling that we want so much more than we have is God speaking to you, because He wants so much more for you too.

On the other hand, instead of a quest for greatness, a testimony of our need for God can be found in feelings of being so insignificant that we fear being swallowed up by the bigness of this world. It can be so overwhelming to have everything out of our control that we realize we need God to be in control. Then there is the feeling of emptiness that can't be appeased by drugs, sex, alcohol, material things, popularity, or success. The feeling of emptiness isn't so quiet but is a God-shaped hole that is actually screaming out loud with anger, anxiety, or depression!

Innate Understanding of Justice

One powerful testimony God has put in our hearts is the realization that there is right and wrong. Regardless what post-modernism suggests, we all know we have been wronged if our girlfriend or husband cheats on us, or if our business partner cleans out our bank account, stealing all the profit! We even know it is wrong when we cheat and steal, and we are left with the horrible feeling of guilt and shame. The Bible says that our conscience is a testimony in us, testifying to the fact that by nature we know there is a God.

> "For when Gentiles, who do not have the law, by nature do what the law requires, they are a law to themselves, even though they do not have the law. They show that the work of the law is written on their hearts, **while their conscience also bears witness, and their conflicting thoughts accuse or even excuse them** on that day when, according to my gospel, God judges the secrets of men by Christ Jesus" (Romans 2:14-16).

When our thoughts excuse or accuse us, there is a "knowing" that we have missed the mark. Even then God is speaking through His Spirit to guide us away from wrong decisions because He created us and knows what is best for our happiness. Sometimes there are consequences for our wrong actions—these too serve to testify that there is an Absolute that we can't deny.

<u>Suffering</u>

What about the problem of suffering? Usually, the question of suffering is used against God: "How could a good God allow suffering?" That question is worthy of discussion and many books have been written on that topic. On the other hand, I noticed in the story of Moses when God sent the ten plagues to Egypt that the purpose for sending evil was actually to have the opposite effect, so people could see that He is a great and powerful God:

> "For this time I will send all my plagues on you yourself, and on your servants and your people, **so that you may know that there is none like me in all the earth.** For by now I could have put out my hand and struck you and your people with pestilence, and you would have been cut off from the earth. But **for this purpose I have raised you up, to show you my power, so that my name may be proclaimed in all the earth**" (Exodus 9:14-16).

God started in the Garden of Eden with a perfect world, a utopia, and even then, His people turned against Him and went their own way. Today, if we lived in a utopia, we would not need God, and God knows how few of us would ever even think of Him. Instead, living in this evil fallen world, every child is given plenty of reasons to know his or her need for someone to rescue and deliver him; a need for a Savior and God's help. As the world continues to become more evil, and we come nearer to the end times prophesied in Scripture; God is allowing evil to multiply evil in the hope of getting our attention, in hope that we will search for Him and seek Him with our whole hearts so that we will find Him.

The promise of Jeremiah 29:13, which many of us know and quote for its awesome promise to give us a wonderful "hope and future," was written on the brink of catastrophe when Israel was being taken into captivity by the Babylonians which ended up being the status quo for 70 years. Even in 70 years of suffering, God was there with Israel, working things out for their good, for them to have a hope and future. Likewise, God is working in suffering to get your attention and draw you to Himself.

> "For thus says the LORD: When seventy years are completed for Babylon, I will visit you, and I will fulfill to you my promise and bring

you back to this place. **For I know the plans I have for you, declares the LORD, plans for welfare and not for evil, to give you a future and a hope. Then you will call upon me and come and pray to me, and I will hear you. You will seek me and find me, when you seek me with all your heart"** (Jeremiah 29:10-13).

According to this passage, finding God is contingent upon our calling on Him, praying to Him, and seeking Him with all our heart. In the New Testament, there is a very interesting passage that tells us that creator God, who has made everything and gives life and breath to humankind, has determined the time and the place we each live so that we would seek Him.

"The God who made the world and everything in it, being Lord of heaven and earth, does not live in temples made by man, nor is he served by human hands, as though he needed anything, since he himself gives to all mankind life and breath and everything. And he made from one man every nation of mankind to live on all the face of the earth, **having determined allotted periods and the boundaries of their dwelling place, that they should seek God, in the hope that they might feel their way toward him and find him. Yet he is actually not far from each one of us for in him we live and move and have our being**" (Acts 17:24-28).

God orchestrates your whole life with one goal, that you might seek Him and "feel your way toward Him and find Him." From the foundation of the world, God's good purpose in creating you was so that you would seek Him and find Him, so that He could have a relationship with you. His promise is that He is not far from any one of us, for it is in Him we actually have life. For God is a God who is near, not far off, He fills the heavens and the earth (see Jeremiah 23:23-24), and the word He is speaking to you today is very near to you, in your heart, so that you can respond to it (see Deuteronomy 30:14). He promises, "Ask, and it will be given to you; seek, and you will find; knock, and it will be opened to you" (Matthew 7:7).

Unfortunately, the Book of Revelation already warns us that even at the end of the world when terrible tribulation comes, people will not seek Him, repent, or give Him glory (see Revelation 16:9, 11). Other verses warn us that even though people know God from His constant speaking to us and have no excuse, many do not glorify or give thanks to Him:

> "For although they knew God, they did not honor him as God or give thanks to him, but they became futile in their thinking, and their foolish hearts were darkened. Claiming to be wise, they became fools, and exchanged the glory of the immortal God for images resembling mortal man and birds and animals and creeping things" (Romans 1:21-22).

Even though God had given us a testimony of Himself throughout the ages, especially in His creation, we have not honored God. These verses say that instead of glorifying the creator God, we have glorified the creation, which has resulted in our lives being futile, foolish, and darkened without meaning or purpose. The futile, foolish, meaninglessness of life in itself is a way God is speaking to us and calling us to Himself. For the consequence of living life without God is a life of emptiness and sorrow which God allows in the hope that we "might seek God, might feel our way toward him" (see Acts 17:27). God's whole purpose in creating us, even before the ages began, was to be in relationship with us. He wants to save us and give us a holy calling, a meaningful destiny, a hope, and a future that can only be found in a relationship with Jesus.

> "So, Jesus again said to them… "I came that they may have life and have it abundantly" (John 10:7, 10).

> "God, who saved us and called us to a holy calling, not because of our works but because of his own purpose and grace, which he gave us in Christ Jesus before the ages began" (2 Timothy 1:9).

God is Calling You to a Love Relationship

The biggest testimony in our lives of God calling us is our need to be loved and in a relationship. People have tried many substitutes and counterfeits to fill this need for love in their lives, but we will never be completely satisfied with any other love relationship because no one else has been designed to completely meet our need for love, nor were we created to meet all of another person's need for love. No matter how wonderful a spouse or significant other is, we are left hungering for more. God has left us hungering and longing for His love in the hope that we would search and find Him. God's desire in calling us is for Him to have us to love and be in a relationship with! According to Scripture, the purpose of God's will in choosing us is His love for us which He proved in sending Jesus Christ, our Beloved.

"He chose us in him before the foundation of the world...In love, he predestined [*or chose*] us for adoption as sons through Jesus Christ, according to the purpose of his will, to the praise of his glorious grace, with which he has blessed us in the Beloved" (Ephesians 1:4-6).

According to these verses, we see that the reason God the Father chose us was to have a love relationship with us as His adopted children. "I will be a father to you, and you shall be sons and daughters to me, says the Lord Almighty" (2 Corinthians 6:18). As our Father, God loves us like His children. Not only that, Jesus loves us and proved it by laying down His life for us out of His love for us. "By this we know love, that he laid down his life for us" (1 John 3:16). Jesus is the lover of our souls and we are His beloved. We belong to Him, and He belongs to us! His desire is for us (see Song of Solomon 6:3, 7:10). How awesome is this!

The Old Testament is a picture of God choosing a people out of love for them. God chose the people of Israel simply because of His love for them, not because of anything they had done to earn it or because of who they were as a people. God's purpose was to exhibit His choosing and loving a random people group, so that even now we would have a picture in history to see God's desire for a relationship. God's interactions with Israel in Scripture revealed that He actually wanted a relationship with them. "For what great nation is there that has a god so near to it as the LORD our God is to us, whenever we call upon him?" (Deuteronomy 4:7). The testimony in Scripture of God's relationship with His people Israel is a model of the relationship He wants with us today. As a people in the Old Testament, Israel was nothing, not bigger or better than any other people group, but they became God's chosen people only because He loved them. This verse could have been written about you even as it was written about the children of Israel. You are God's chosen treasure because He loves you.

"For you are a people holy to the LORD your God. **The LORD your God has chosen you to be a people for his treasured possession,** out of all the peoples who are on the face of the earth. **It was not because you were more in number than any other people that the LORD set his love on you and chose you, for you were the fewest of all peoples, but it is because the LORD loves you**" (Deuteronomy 7:6-8).

The history of the people of Israel shows us the one and only true God who is love. Moses at one point asked God to see His glory. In response to Moses' request, God defined His own glory by describing His love and compassion for us.

The glory of God is that He loves us and wants a relationship with us, and that He is abounding in steadfast love and faithfulness towards us.

> "The LORD passed before him and proclaimed, "**The LORD, the LORD, a God merciful and gracious, slow to anger, and abounding in steadfast love and faithfulness**, keeping steadfast love for thousands, forgiving iniquity and transgression and sin" (Exodus 34:6-7).

The glory of God is that He abounds in mercy, grace, love, and faithfulness; and that He is slow to anger and forgives our sins—a love that is completely unconditional and meets our needs perfectly! Throughout history, God announced His love to His people, a love that has no beginning and no end but is everlasting, eternal. God has drawn His chosen ones to Himself with loving-kindness, and is abounding in steadfast love and compassion to those who fear Him.

> "I have loved you with an **everlasting love**; therefore, I have drawn you with **loving-kindness**" (Jeremiah 31:3 NASV).

> "The LORD is merciful and gracious; slow to anger and **abounding in steadfast love**. He will not always chide, nor will he keep his anger forever. He does not deal with us according to our sins, nor repay us according to our iniquities. **For as high as the heavens are above the earth, so great is his steadfast love toward those who fear him**; as far as the east is from the west, so far does he remove our transgressions from us. As a father shows compassion to his children, so the LORD shows compassion to those who fear him" (Psalm 103:8-13).

In the New Testament, God actually defines Himself as love. God demonstrated His love to us by sending Jesus to bring salvation and life to the world of people who did not know or love God. Jesus's life, death, and resurrection are proof of God's love for you!

> "**God shows His love for us** in that while we were still sinners, Christ died for us" (Romans 5:8).

> "**By this we know love**; that he laid down his life for us" (1 John 3:16).

> "**God is love. In this the love of God was made manifest among us, that God sent his only Son into the world, so that we might live

through him. In this is love, not that we have loved God but that he loved us and sent his Son" (1 John 4:8-10).

God's love for you and His desire for a relationship with you is the purpose for which you were created. You are the object of God's love. There is much in Scripture written about the love of God for you. His love surpasses all understanding because it is so much bigger than we can comprehend.

"So that Christ may dwell in your hearts through faith—that you, being rooted and grounded in love, may have strength to comprehend with all the saints what is the breadth and length and height and depth, and **to know the love of Christ that surpasses knowledge**, that you may be filled with all the fullness of God" (Ephesians 3:17-19).

"Who shall separate us from the love of Christ? Shall tribulation, or distress, or persecution, or famine, or nakedness, or danger, or sword? ...No, in all these things we are more than conquerors through him who loved us. **For I am sure that neither death nor life, nor angels nor rulers, nor things present nor things to come, nor powers, nor height nor depth, nor anything else in all creation, will be able to separate us from the love of God in Christ Jesus our Lord**" (Romans 8:35-39).

This God, who sent Jesus to reveal Himself to us, is the only God who has left heaven and taken the initiative to pursue a relationship with the human race. He is the only God who has provided a means of dealing with our sin, guilt, and ungodliness by taking our punishment and reconciling us to Him. He is the only God who defines Himself as love and created us for relationship with Him. No other God calls Himself Love, Savior, Father, and calls us His dear children. He is the only God who is coming again to rescue us from the suffering of this earth and take us to be with Himself forever!

All of us have a need for love at the core of who we are. We were created with that need as the recipient of God's love. We will always be longing to be loved until we find the love of God for us. Even the love of family and friends will fall short of meeting this need for love that is deep within our soul. Only God can satisfy you. We were made to be loved by God, and until we receive His love and know how broad, long, high, and deep His love is for us, we will never be satisfied. His love for us is so big and great it goes beyond our ability to comprehend it. Nothing can separate us from the love of God. No problems, no powers, nor anything created can separate us from the love of God which is found in Christ Jesus. God's love is the love your heart has been longing for. Only the love of God will satisfy the longing of your heart. God is calling you to a love relationship with Him which He proved by sending Christ Jesus to save you.

CHAPTER 1 Questions for Thought and Discussion

1. Will we have an excuse on judgment day for not knowing God? Why or why not?

2. List four ways explained in the chapter that God has tried to get your attention.

3. What did Jesus' life on earth reveal about God the Father?

4. a) How does the Bible reveal who Jesus and God the Father is?

   b) Why does the Bible say that it can be trusted?

5. a) According to Acts 17:24-28 (page 6), why did God create us?

   b) What did He predetermine for you?

6. a) What would a "love relationship with God" mean or look like to you?

   b) What would be different if you really believed that God loved you?

   c) What problems in your life are because you don't believe that God loves you or is calling you into relationship with Him?

CHAPTER 2

Chosen by God

"**He chose us** in him before the foundation of the world" (Ephesians 1:4).

God said of the prophet Jeremiah, "Before I formed you in the womb I knew you, and before you were born, I consecrated you" (Jeremiah 1:4). The Apostle Paul said of himself that God "set me apart before I was born, and who called me by his grace" (Galatians 1: 15). You too were known and consecrated by God, and set apart before you were even born! God designed the blueprint for who you would be and the purpose He has for you. He is the one who holds the keys to your destiny! If you wonder what you were created for and what your purpose is, God is the one who holds the blueprint; even to this day. No matter what has come against you, and how many years you have not pursued your destiny, nothing is lost; it is with God. God has a holy calling for you. "Holy" means, "a set-apart life" that only you can fulfill; a life that is set apart for the purpose of God.

> "God, who saved us and **called us to a holy calling**, not because of our works but because of his own purpose and grace, which he gave us in Christ Jesus before the ages began" (2 Timothy 1:9).

God has chosen you, not because of your works, but because of "His own purpose and grace." God chose you "before the foundation of the world," "before the ages began" when you could have absolutely nothing to do with it! No possibility to earn being chosen by your good works. Jesus said, "You did not choose me, but I chose you" (John 15:16). Even the response we make to Jesus is just a function of His calling and choosing us. Jesus also said, "No one can come to me unless the Father who sent me draws him" (John 6:44). What a miracle to hear God's voice and to sense His drawing you. All you have to do is respond to Him, "Today, if you hear his voice, do not harden your hearts!" (Hebrews 3:7, 15).

Foreknown By God

You were on God's mind "before the ages began." "He chose us in him before the foundation of the world" (Ephesians 1:4). It was God's thoughts that designed the blueprint of who you would be, and it was God who shaped and formed you in the secret place long before you were conceived. It was God who wove you together in the depths of the earth. It was God who knit you together in your mother's womb. His eyes were on you before you were even formed. You may or may not have been "planned" by your parents, but your heavenly Father planned, designed, and created you before the world began. He wanted you on this earth at this time in history for His purposes. He has a destiny and calling for your life. You are fearfully and wonderfully made! You are God-the-Father's child and beautiful in His eyes!

> "For you formed my inward parts; you knitted me together in my mother's womb. I praise you, for I am fearfully and wonderfully made. Wonderful are your works; my soul knows it very well. My frame was not hidden from you, when I was being made in secret, intricately woven in the depths of the earth. Your eyes saw my unformed substance" (Psalm 139:13-16).

In fact, His plans for you are too many to count, and He is always thinking thoughts about you, even to this day. His thoughts of you are vast in number, more numerous than the sand on the seashore, and all of them are loving and precious. From the foundation of the world, God not only saw to it that you were wonderfully made, but He has written a book about every day that you will live on the face of this earth. Before any of your days began, God has written every day down in His book. He knows you better than you know yourself! "Even the hairs of your head are all numbered" (Matthew 10:30).

> "In your book were written, every one of them, the days that were formed for me, when as yet there was none of them. How precious to me are your thoughts, O God! How vast is the sum of them! If I would count them, they are more than the sand. I awake, and I am still with you." (Psalm 139:16-18).

The same Psalm tells us that God knows when you sit down and get up, He knows your thoughts, and He knows your path and is intimately acquainted with all of your ways. He knows what you are going to say before you say it. God knows everything about you! In fact, He goes before you and at the same time follows you with His hand on you. God even knew all the mistakes you would make. He knew all the things you would regret and hate about yourself. He knew that you would spend years going your own way without thinking about Him—...and yet He still loved you, called you, and chose you to be His own.

> "O LORD, you have searched me and known me! You know when I sit down and when I rise up; you discern my thoughts from afar. You search out my path and my lying down and are acquainted with all my ways. Even before a word is on my tongue, behold, O LORD, you know it altogether. You hem me in, behind and before, and lay your hand upon me. Such knowledge is too wonderful for me; it is high; I cannot attain it" (Psalm 139:1-6).

You can't hide. There is nowhere you can go from God! Even if you feel like you are living in "Sheol," which in Scripture is a place of death and suffering, God is with you! Even before you know God, He knew you and His hand was leading and guiding you, His powerful right hand holds you. Even if you have made choices to dwell in the darkness, God sees you and His light makes the darkness visible (see Ephesians 5:13).

> "Where shall I go from your Spirit? Or where shall I flee from your presence? If I ascend to heaven, you are there! If I make my bed in Sheol, you are there! If I take the wings of the morning and dwell in the uttermost parts of the sea, even there your hand shall lead me, and your right hand shall hold me. If I say, "Surely the darkness shall cover me, and the light about me be night," even the darkness is not dark to you; the night is bright as the day, for darkness is as light with you" (Psalm 139:7-12).

The kind of relationship God-the-Father wants to have with you is as close as a perfect Father-child relationship. "In love he predestined us for adoption as sons through Jesus Christ" (Ephesians 1:5). God's will and plan for you is to orchestrate your whole life so that you would be His child. Some of us, due to the fallen-ness of the world, do not have a good picture of a father-child relationship; nothing like the relationship that is possible to have with God. God is the perfect Father! He wants to be a perfect Father to you and to meet every father-need that you may have. God the Father is your provider, who "provides everything we need for life and godliness" (2 Peter 1:3), and "who has blessed us in Christ with every spiritual blessing in the heavenly places" (Ephesians 1:3). Since the foundation of the world, God has prepared an eternal Kingdom for you with Him (see Matthew

25:34). Even when Jesus spoke of heaven, He described it as a place of relationship, where He can take you to Himself and where you can be with Him.

> "Let not your hearts be troubled. Believe in God; believe also in me. In my Father's house are many rooms. If it were not so, would I have told you that I go to prepare a place for you? And if I go and prepare a place for you, I will come again and **will take you to myself, that where I am you may be also**" (John 14:1-3).

God the Father wants a relationship with you, is pursuing you, and wants to reveal Himself to you. God knew all the good things that would come your way, but He also knew all the hardships you would suffer. He knew the evil and instability in the world you would have to face. As Father, His commitment to you is to ultimately save you, rescue and deliver you from evil and, in the end, work all things together for your good.

> "We know that for those who love God **all things work together for good**, for those who are called according to his purpose" (Romans 8:28).

Regardless of what has come against you, Father God knows that His purpose for you will prevail because as your Creator, He holds your blueprint, which He designed from the foundation of the world. He knows He is able to fulfill His purpose for you.

> "I cry out to God Most High, to **God who fulfills His purpose for me**" (Psalm 57:2).

> "Though I walk in the midst of trouble, you preserve my life;
> you stretch out your hand against the wrath of my enemies,
> and your right hand delivers me. **The LORD will fulfill his purpose for me;** your steadfast love, O LORD, endures forever" (Psalm 138:8-9).

God's purpose for you is good! "For I know the plans I have for you, declares the LORD, plans for welfare and not for evil, to give you a future and a hope" (Jeremiah 29:11). As a good Father, His purpose in restoring relationship with you is to give you a destiny of future and hope.

> "He predestined us for adoption as sons through Jesus Christ, according to the purpose of his will" (Ephesians 1:5).

God's purpose to restore relationship with us and to give us a hope and a future is only found in Jesus Christ. This is the mystery that we will discover in this book.

"Making known to us **the mystery of his will, according to his purpose, which he set forth in Christ**" (Ephesians 1:9).

"This was according to the **eternal purpose** that he has realized **in Christ Jesus our Lord**" (Ephesians 3:11).

God, His many thoughts of you, His purpose and destiny for your life, and Christ Jesus may seem like a mystery to you; and you may be right because the Bible says that there actually are mysteries that date back to the foundation of the world. It is God who is in charge of the times and seasons of life, and it is God who reveals the deep and hidden things to us for He alone knows the mysteries that are in the dark. God promises to give wisdom to those who are wise and knowledge to those who have enough understanding to seek God for those things which are a mystery.

"Blessed be the name of God forever and ever,
to whom belong wisdom and might.
He changes times and seasons;
he removes kings and sets up kings;
he gives wisdom to the wise
and knowledge to those who have understanding;
he reveals deep and hidden things;
he knows what is in the darkness,
and the light dwells with him" (Daniel 2:20-22).

The good news is that if you seek Him, it is possible for you to begin to know and understand the amazing thoughts of God about you and to see the mysteries that only He can reveal to you. "It is the glory of God to conceal a matter; it is the glory of kings to search it out" (Proverbs 25:2). One of our pastors, Pastor Dennis Arnold, used to tell the youth at our church, "God has given you a destiny that you know not of." He challenged them to make the effort to seek God and find out what their destiny was. I'm challenging you to find the relationship God wants with you, and His good plans and purposes for you. He has a destiny for you that you know not of. It will be your glory to search it out!

For The Glory of Christ in Us

> "But you are a chosen race, a royal priesthood, a holy nation, a people **for his own possession, that you may proclaim the excellencies** of him who called you out of darkness into his marvelous light. Once you were not a people, but now you are **God's people**; once you had not received mercy, but now you have received mercy" (1 Peter 2:9-10).

This passage declares that God is calling out a chosen race, a royal priesthood, and a holy nation to be a people for God's own possession. Have you ever thought of yourself as highly as God—chosen, royal, holy? God has such a high calling for all of His chosen ones! God wants a people for His own possession, for the love relationship we have just discussed. God's purpose for everyone He created and called is that He would be glorified in us. According to the *Westminster Catechism*, "Man's chief end is to glorify God and enjoy Him forever." God is the one who calls us out of darkness and shines the marvelous light of His glory on us. He is the one who takes us from being nothing and makes us a royal people of His own, all because of His mercy. Mercy is defined as God's attitude of pity and compassion for the ills of those in need or distress, with the ability, resources, and action to meet those needs. Though we were a mess, completely needy with nothing to offer God, God saw fit to rescue us and make us His chosen people, who would bring Him glory. He wants to take the least of us, the biggest messes, and make us to be a chosen race, a royal priesthood, and a holy nation. God's chosen ones glorify Him by becoming who He makes us to be.

> "Everyone who is called by my name, whom **I created for my glory**, whom I formed and made" (Isaiah 43:7).
> "**The Lord gives grace and glory**. No good thing does He withhold from those who walk uprightly" (Psalm 84:11).

God created us in His image. "Then God said, "Let us make man in our image, after our likeness" (Genesis 1:26). God created humans different from all the other living beings on the earth. Adam and Eve were created wondrously in His image, and He breathed His Spirit into them. As a creation of God, you have the potential of declaring the glory of God just because He made you and you are fearfully and wonderfully made in His likeness. You are awesome in His eyes and He loves you as His own creation and expression of His own image. You are the reflection of God's image that He takes pleasure in. Just like a mother or father, He is honored when He sees His image in you, reflecting His glory. He is delighted when He sees you being who He created you to be.

Before Adam and Eve fell, it was God's Spirit living in Adam and Eve that emanated God's glory, but because of sin, we lost God's Spirit and His glory in us. We no longer could be all that He created us to be. The Bible says that, "all have sinned and fall short of the glory of God" (Romans 3:23). Since Jesus' death on the cross, we can now hope to have God's glory restored by Christ Jesus living in us, restoring His glorious Spirit in and through us. "Christ in you, the hope of glory" (Colossians 1:27). Until we come into relationship with God, we may not feel very glorious, and in and of ourselves we are not glorious, but when we invite Christ Jesus into our life, it is Jesus in us that gives us His glory. The Bible says that we are like jars of clay, by ourselves there is no glory; we are nothing but clay. The glory comes from inviting the glory of Jesus Christ in us. God is actually glorifying Himself with the glory which Jesus reflects in us.

> "For God, who said, 'Let light shine out of darkness,' **has shone in our hearts to give the light of the knowledge of the glory of God in the face of Jesus Christ. But we have this treasure in jars of clay, to show that the surpassing power belongs to God and not to us**" (2 Corinthians 4:6-7).

> "Now in a great house there are not only vessels of gold and silver but also of wood and clay, some for honorable use, some for dishonorable. Therefore, **if anyone cleanses himself from what is dishonorable, he will be a vessel for honorable use,** set apart as holy, useful to the master of the house, ready for every good work" (2 Timothy 2:20-21).

We all know that we are just a clay pot, from dust we have been made and to dust we will return (see Genesis 3:19), but at the same time we have testimony within ourselves that we want to be created for glory, for some honorable glorious use! We want to live for something more than mundane day-in-day-out survival. We want more glory than just focusing on our pain, wants, and needs, or living for our selfish pleasures. We long to exist for something great, to have a life that has meaning; to live our life with a purpose! I submit to you that living for the glory of God is the wonder of God that we were created for from the foundation of the earth. God is worthy of nothing less than this! Because we are made in His image, we will not be satisfied with anything less than His glory filling us. Christ Jesus in us is our only hope for true glory!

> "To them God chose to make known how great among the Gentiles are the riches of the glory of **this mystery, which is Christ in you**, the hope of glory" (Colossians 1:27).

The glory of Jesus Christ in us gives us purpose and meaning for life; a life worth living. When we invite Jesus into our life and decide to become His follower, we become part of His Kingdom on earth where He rules and reigns in victory. The reality is that as His followers, we are on the winning side in the epic battle on earth between good and evil, between God and Satan which will be explained in the following chapters. As Jesus' people, we occupy the world which will one day be turned over to the rule and reign of Jesus, the King of kings and Lord of lords. The glory of Christ in us is that we are part of Jesus' Kingdom that will not suffer defeat, but has conquered evil by Jesus' death on the cross. Jesus will reign triumphant throughout eternity. We are called to a destiny to share in the glory of Christ Jesus in us and us living victoriously in Him.

The Glory of Being Called and Chosen by God

"Having the eyes of your hearts enlightened, **that you may know what is the hope to which he has called you, what are the riches of his glorious inheritance in the saints**" (Ephesians 1:18).

We, the saints, are chosen ones. What does "the saints" mean? Rather than meaning people who live perfect lives; "saints" or "holy ones" actually means "set apart ones" who have set themselves apart for God and have a relationship with Him. They are those who have given up making themselves their own god and chasing after the things of this world, in order to align themselves with Jesus and chase after a relationship with Him. Some of you may be wondering how this applies to you when you do not yet have a relationship with Jesus. Romans 11:29 says, "For the gifts and the calling of God are irrevocable." God is calling you and His call is irrevocable whether you receive it or not. God has called the whole world, "For God so loved the world, that he gave his only Son, that whoever believes in him should not perish but have eternal life" (John 3:16). God "desires all people to be saved and to come to the knowledge of the truth" (1 Timothy 2:4). Unfortunately, many have not even heard the good news of God's love and calling. Others have heard of God's calling but it has not been presented to them in love, so they have been turned-off and are not interested in fulfilling their calling. God says "For many are called, but few are chosen" (Matthew 22:14). The difference between being "called" and "chosen" is that God calls everyone, but only those who respond to God's call are the chosen ones. Those who respond to the call of God by giving your full allegiance to Jesus as your Savior and Lord, instead of yourself or the world, are the chosen ones.

When we find our calling to be in a love relationship with God and walk out our glorious place in His Kingdom, there is nothing more fulfilling and satisfying. When we become a child of the King of Kings and grow into who we were meant to be since the foundation of the world, we will be living the life that is truly living! To know who we are in Christ Jesus and to know our calling is a glorious way to live life. Christ living His life in us enables us to be who we were created to be. We were created to walk out a calling which God purposed from the foundation of the world. When God sees us walking in our calling, He is pleased, and at the same time, when we find our calling and walk in it, there is nothing more thrilling for us. The only way to know your calling is to connect with your Creator. He is the one who holds the blueprint to your life. The only way to walk out your calling is in relationship with God in whom "we live and move and have our being" (Acts 17:28). In relationship with God, we fulfill the calling we were created for, which gives us a glorious life that glorifies God in us. It completes a circuit which allows the love and power of God to flow gloriously thorough us to the world and back to God, which glorifies Him.

His calling and good plans for us included specific good works which He prepared beforehand for us to walk in; works that would be the perfect fit for who He created us to be. Since God is our Creator, He knows what He has designed us to be and do. We have the freedom to make our own choices, but we will never feel as fulfilled and satisfied as when we are fulfilling the call of God on our life. The call of God on our life starts with being fulfilled in a love relationship with God, but it is also worked out in who God has created us to be and what He has prepared for us to do. As we walk out the works God has planned for us, others will see the glory in us fulfilling our calling that will bring God glory.

> "For we are his workmanship, **created in Christ Jesus for good works, which God prepared beforehand, that we should walk in them**" (Ephesians 2:10).

> "To this end we always pray for you, **that our God may make you worthy of his calling and may fulfill every resolve for good and every work of faith by his power, so that the name of our Lord Jesus may be glorified in you, and you in him**, according to the grace of our God and the Lord Jesus Christ" (2 Thessalonians 1:11-12).

God is calling and choosing you out of love, offering you salvation and has prepared good works for you to walk in so that Jesus would be glorified in you and you would be glorified in Him. All this was God's plan and His thoughts for you since the foundation of the world. Up until now, God has done it all for you. He is calling you without you initiating anything, so now what is your part? Simply to respond— to receive the gift of His love in Christ Jesus and to make a decision to give your life to Jesus as Lord who is your only hope of glory.

> "To whom God willed to make known what is the riches of the glory of this mystery among the Gentiles, which is **Christ in you, the hope of glory**" (Colossians 1:27)

> "Therefore, brothers, **be all the more diligent to make your calling and election [choosing] sure**, for if you practice these qualities, you will never fall. For in this way there will be richly provided for you an entrance into the eternal kingdom of our Lord and Savior Jesus Christ" (2 Peter 1:10-11).

CHAPTER 2 Questions for Thought and Discussion

1. What implications or what conclusions can you draw from the statement "God chose you in Him before the foundation of the world?" (Ephesians 1:4)

2. Psalm 139 says that you are "fearfully and wonderfully made," that "God knows everything about you," and that "God is always with you." Which of those three facts about God is most needed or important to you right now and why?

3. To be a child of God brings up our earthly understanding of a parent child relationship.

   a) How is God the Father like your parents?

   b) How is He different from your parents?

4. How do you put your perspective of your earthly father on to the heavenly Father?

5. God has a good purpose for your life and good works for you to do that are glorious!
a) Do you know what your purpose and destiny is?

b) How could you find out what your purpose and destiny is?

6. a) What does it mean to you to be chosen by God?

b) How would you feel differently or what would you do differently if you believed that you are chosen by God for a relationship with Him, and that He has a good purpose and destiny for you?

CHAPTER 3

Going Your Own Way

"To bring to light for everyone what is the plan of **the mystery hidden for ages in God** who created all things" (Ephesians 3:9).

"**The mystery hidden for ages and generations** but now revealed to his saints" (Colossians 1:26).

So, if before the foundation of the world, God chose you and created you for a relationship with Him, if He loves you, and if He has called you to have a life of purpose that glorifies Him, what happened? Why is God so hard to find? Why are our lives so disconnected from God? Where's the glory? To answer these questions, we have to start with some of the mysteries of the foundation of the world. Earlier we talked about the mysteries that are hidden in God from the foundation of the world. There are mysteries we do not know regarding what happened before the beginning of the world when only God existed, as He has existed for eternity past and has no beginning. Then there are mysteries that established the world's order, laws governing the spirit realm, and the boundaries of good and evil on the earth, which we can only know in part. We will never fully know many of these mysteries until we are with Jesus in heaven where we can spend eternity learning about the things of God. Millenniums into eternity, we still will never exhaust the possibilities of knowing God better.

Some of the mysteries of the world have been made known to us by God in the Scriptures. There is one mystery that happened before the beginning of the world that Isaiah 14 tells us about. Satan had been created as a beautiful angel: he was a leader among angels and in charge of worship in the heavenly realm. Unfortunately, he was prideful about his beauty and worship and wanted to become like God Himself:

"You said in your heart, 'I will ascend to heaven; above the stars of God, I will set my throne on high; I will sit on the mount of assembly in the far reaches of the north; I will ascend above the heights of the clouds; I will make myself like the Most High'" (Isaiah 14:13-14).

His punishment for treason was to be cast down from heaven to the earth, along with one third of the angels who followed him (see Revelation 12:4). Even Jesus recalled, "I saw Satan fall like lightning from heaven" (Luke 10:18). While on the earth, Satan "made the world like a desert" (Isaiah 14:17), so that "the earth was without form and void, and darkness was over the face of the deep" (Genesis 1:2). So, before "the beginning" the state of the earth while Satan ruled it had become void, dark and empty (see Genesis 1:2). Then the Spirit of God began to hover over the face of the earth (see Genesis 1:2); God the Father began to create the entire world with the word of His mouth, making everything through Jesus Christ (see Genesis 1:3-31).

Scripture declares that Jesus Christ is not only the baby born in Bethlehem who died on the cross, rose from the dead, and lives today, but Jesus was also the God of creation. When God said, "let us make" (Genesis 1:26), He was talking to Jesus "by whom all things were made" (John 1:3) and the Holy Spirit who was "hovering over the face of the earth" (Genesis 1:2).

"He [Jesus Christ] is the image of the invisible God, the firstborn of all creation. **For by him all things were created, in heaven and on earth, visible and invisible, whether thrones or dominions or rulers or authorities—all things were created through him and for him.** And he is before all things, and in him all things hold together" (Colossians 1:15-17).

"His Son, whom he appointed the heir of all things, through whom **also he created the world.** He is the radiance of the glory of God and the exact imprint of his nature, and he upholds the universe by the word of his power" (Hebrews 1:2-3).

In the following passage, Jesus is called "the Word," and the following verses state that Jesus was with God in the beginning, and everything in the world was created by the same Jesus, the Word, who approximately 4000 years later, became flesh and dwelt among us as the only Son of God.

"In the beginning was the Word, and the Word was with God, and the Word was God. He was in the beginning with God. **All things were**

made through him, and without him was not anything made that was made. In him was life, and the life was the light of men…. And the Word became flesh and dwelt among us, and we have seen his glory, glory as of the only Son from the Father, full of grace and truth" (John 1:1-4, 14).

Creation

"Then God said, "Let there be light"; and there was light. God saw that the light was good; and God separated the light from the darkness. God called the light day, and the darkness He called night. And there was evening and there was morning, one day" (Genesis 1:3-5).

When God began creation, the first thing He created was light, which He called day, and darkness, which He called night. It is significant to note that according to the Bible, creation did not take millions of years. The Bible clearly says that a day was defined on the first day as morning and evening so that at the end of every day of creation, it is stated "and there was evening and there was morning" the first day, the second day, third day, fourth day, etc. so that creation took six 24-hour days and on the seventh day, God rested. Another interesting thing to note from Scripture is that all the animals were each made "according to their kinds" rather than evolving into other animals over a period of millions of years (see Genesis 1:24-25).

"And God said, 'Let the earth bring forth living creatures **according to their kinds**—livestock and creeping things and beasts of the earth **according to their kinds.**' And it was so. And God made the beasts of the earth **according to their kinds** and the livestock **according to their kinds**, and everything that creeps on the ground **according to its kind.** And God saw that it was good… And God saw everything that he had made, and behold, it was very good. **And there was evening and there was morning, the sixth day**" (Genesis 1:24-25, 31).

Human beings, according to the Bible, were created in God's image as male and female, and they also did not evolve from primate beginnings.

"Then God said, 'Let us make man in our image, after our likeness.' So, God created man in his own image, in the image of God he created him; **male and female he created them**" (Genesis 1:26-27).

When God created human beings, He immediately declared their purpose and that was for them to rule the world; to have dominion over everything God had created. This is the really important point in regards to what happened to God's plan and purpose for our lives. Up until the creation of the world, Satan had ruled the world with chaos and destruction. Then, in the beginning of the world, God established a new order that set man to rule and have dominion over everything He had created. We can only imagine how enraged Satan was to have God usurp his rule on earth and give it to human beings. Enter the original antagonist and protagonist from which all stories have their origin!

> "And **let them have dominion** over the fish of the sea and over the birds of the heavens and over the livestock and over all the earth and over every creeping thing that creeps on the earth" (Genesis 1:26).

> "When I look at your heavens, the work of your fingers,
> the moon and the stars, which you have set in place,
> what is man that you are mindful of him,
> and the son of man that you care for him?
> **Yet you have made him a little lower than the heavenly beings
> and crowned him with glory and honor.
> You have given him dominion over the works of your hands;
> you have put all things under his feet,**
> all sheep and oxen, and also the beasts of the field,
> the birds of the heavens, and the fish of the sea,
> whatever passes along the paths of the seas" (Psalm 8:3-8).

The Fall

One of the mysteries that was established from the foundation of the world but not told us in Scripture is how this conflict between Satan, the antagonist, and Adam and Eve, the protagonists, came into being. We can only imagine Satan approaching God, challenging Him for dominion over the world and the following wager being made. God would put man in a perfect garden and man would have perfect communion with God; the only limitation would be the eating the fruit of one tree in the middle of the Garden of Eden. Man was placed in authority over the garden, all the plants and all the animals; he even got to name them. The only thing he was not allowed was to eat the fruit of the tree in the middle of the garden, the Tree of the Knowledge of Good and Evil. With such ideal circumstances, what were the chances that man would eat from the tree in the middle of the garden? The wager, assumedly, was that if Satan could get man to eat of the fruit of the Tree of the Knowledge of Good and Evil, man would lose control and Satan would regain dominion and authority of the world.

> "The LORD God took the man and put him in the Garden of Eden to work it and keep it. And the LORD God commanded the man, saying, 'You may surely eat of every tree of the garden, but of the tree of the knowledge of good and evil you shall not eat, for in the day that you eat of it you shall surely die'" (Genesis 2:15-17).

The Bible doesn't tell us how long Adam and Eve lived in fellowship with God before Satan was able to tempt them into eating the fruit, but one day Satan came to Eve in the form of a serpent and began to talk to her. Apparently, animals could talk before the Fall because Eve was not surprised by a snake talking to her!

> "But the serpent said to the woman, **'You will not surely die. For God knows that when you eat of it your eyes will be opened, and you will be like God, knowing good and evil.'** So, when the woman saw that the tree was good for food, and that it was a delight to the eyes, and that the tree was to be desired to make one wise, she took of its fruit and ate, and she also gave some to her husband who was with her, and he ate" (Genesis 3:4-6).

Satan used the same temptation to tempt Adam and Eve by which he himself had fallen! They too fell for the temptation that they could become like God! Satan's ploy was to tell Eve that if they disobeyed God and ate the fruit of the Tree of the Knowledge of Good and Evil, they would not die but they would be like God, knowing good and evil. Being like God apparently appealed to Eve and Adam and they ate the fruit. From that moment on, everything changed. Whereas before they only knew "good," now as a result of disobeying God they came to know "evil" as well. Whereas before the Holy Spirit lived in them and filled their spirits, souls, and bodies, they were now left naked and empty. Whereas before they knew the Father's love and sought a relationship with Him, now in shame they hid from Him. Instead of communing with the wisdom and knowledge of God in their spirits to make decisions, they were left with trying to discern good from evil by the knowledge of their own minds. God's warning that "for in the day that you eat of it you shall surely die" (Genesis 2:17) came true, for on that day their spirits were no longer alive with the Spirit of the living God, but dead. Soon after, God cursed them with physical death as well.

"By the sweat of your face you shall eat bread, till you return to the ground, for out of it you were taken; for you are dust, and to dust you shall return" (Genesis 3:19).

More than that, before the Fall, man had dominion over the garden and the animals. Now Satan had taken that dominion back and became ruler of the whole world again. Since mankind's sin separated them from God and they were spiritually dead, they became easy prey for the power of the devil who now could work through mankind's disobedience to bring back chaos and destruction to the earth.

"We know that...**the whole world lies in the power of the evil one**" (1 John 5:19).

"And you were dead in the trespasses and sins in which you once walked, following the course of this world, **following the prince of the power of the air, the spirit that is now at work in the sons of disobedience**—among whom we all once lived in the passions of our flesh, carrying out the desires of the body and the mind, and were by nature children of wrath, like the rest of mankind" (Ephesians 2:1-3).

Generational Consequences

Unfortunately, one of the mystery laws in place from the beginning was that Adam and Eve's disobedience would have an effect on every generation after them. Generation after generation of children has been born into the kingdom of this world ruled by Satan. The consequences of Satan's rule are that sin, disobedience to God, and death have been passed down from Adam and Eve to every generation since the Fall. Since the Fall, we have all lost our calling and destiny which God had designed from before the foundation of the world.

"Therefore, just as **sin came into the world through one man, and death through sin, and so death spread to all men because all sinned**" (Romans 5:12).

"For as **by a man came death**, by a man has come also the resurrection of the dead. **For as in Adam all die**, so also in Christ shall all be made alive" (1 Corinthians 15:21-22).

All mankind is doomed to a life of sin and, consequently, God's wrath and punishment until another human could stand the test of Satan's temptation by resisting sin, choosing to obey God's will perfectly, taking the punishment of God's judgment against sin on our behalf, and conquering the curse of death by rising from the dead. This is exactly what Christ Jesus did, but now we are getting ahead of ourselves.

> "For if, **because of one man's trespass, death reigned through that one man**, much more will those who receive the abundance of grace and the free gift of righteousness reign in life through the one-man Jesus Christ. Therefore, **as one trespassed to condemnation for all men,** so one act of righteousness leads to justification and life for all men. **For as by the one man's disobedience the many were made sinners**, so by the one man's obedience the many will be made righteous" (Romans 5:17-19).

Sin Defined

> "All we like sheep have gone astray; we have turned—**every one to his own way**; and the LORD has laid on him the iniquity of us all" (Isaiah 53:6).

"Sin," or "iniquity" which is the state of being in sin into which we have all been born, according to the above verse, is defined as going our own way rather than going God's way. Anything that does not please God but is pleasing ourselves is sin. Sin involves not just breaking the Ten Commandments, but also involves any way that we are not following God's purpose and destiny for our lives. For generation after generation since Adam, mankind has gone its own way. At Creation, Adam and Eve chose to go their own way by eating the fruit of the Tree of the Knowledge of Good and Evil. Before the flood, God saw that man's thoughts were continually evil, so He decided to destroy everyone, except Noah's family, with a flood.

> "The LORD saw that the wickedness of man was great in the earth, and that **every intention of the thoughts of his heart was only evil continually**. And the LORD was sorry that he had made man on the earth, and it grieved him to his heart. So, the LORD said, "I will blot out man whom I have created from the face of the land, man and animals and creeping things and birds of the heavens, for I am sorry that I have

made them." But Noah found favor in the eyes of the LORD" (Genesis 6:5-8).

In the days of the Judges, the Bible says that, "Everyone did what was right in his own eyes" (Judges 21:25). Psalm 14 says:

"The LORD looks down from heaven on the children of man,
to see if there are any who understand, who seek after God.
**They have all turned aside; together they have become corrupt;
there is none who does good, not even one**" (Psalm 14:2-3).

Isaiah tells us that it is our sins that have separated us from God, and therefore He has hidden His face from us and does not hear.

"Behold, the LORD's hand is not shortened, that it cannot save,
or his ear dull, that it cannot hear; but **your iniquities have made a separation between you and your God, and your sins have hidden his face from you so that he does not hear**" (Isaiah 59:1-2).

In the 60's, everyone "did their own thing;" in the 80's "if it felt good, we did it." Now, in the "post–modern era," we have "tolerance" so we think we can each re-construct our own philosophy as to what is wrong or right for ourselves. According to post-modern thought, there is no longer an absolute right or wrong; now we can each go our own way and do what is right within our own eyes. What we have done, in fact, is made ourselves our own god and fallen prey to the same temptation as the Devil, Adam, and Eve—to want to become like God. We have each gone our own way and our sin has separated us from God.

"For **although they knew God, they did not honor him as God or give thanks to him**, but they became futile in their thinking, and their foolish hearts were darkened. Claiming to be wise, they became fools, and exchanged the glory of the immortal God for images resembling mortal man . . . **they exchanged the truth about God for a lie and worshiped and served the creature rather than the Creator**, who is blessed forever! Amen" (Romans 1:21-23, 25).

According to Scripture, this applies to all of us. We all have gone our own way and have ignored God's way. "All have sinned and fall short of the glory of God" (Romans 3:23). "If we say we have not sinned, we make him a liar, and his word is not in us" (1 John 1:10). Like Adam and Eve, we all suffer with the guilt and shame of sin. Like Adam and Eve, we no longer see just good, we also see the evil of sin every day all around us. We feel empty and separated from God and yet hide from Him. We struggle with what to do with ourselves as we discern with the limits of our own mind. Our spirits are dead, yearning and longing for life; while we live in fear of physical death and our bodies all bear the signs of our mortality. It is sin and these consequences of the Fall that have separated us from God, stolen our purpose and calling, keep us falling short of the glory of God, and kills us in the end. The consequences of sin are spiritual, physical, and eternal death.

Consequences of Sin is Death

"Therefore, just as sin came into the world through one man, and **death through sin, and so death spread to all men because all sinned**…So that, as sin reigned in death, grace also might reign through righteousness leading to eternal life through Jesus Christ our Lord" (Romans 5:12, 21).

"For **the wages of sin is death**, but the free gift of God is eternal life in Christ Jesus our Lord" (Romans 6:23).

The day Adam and Eve sinned; they faced spiritual death as the devil had stolen their relationship with God and killed their spirits so that they were spiritually dead. Satan stole the blessed life in the garden that was once theirs and now they were destined to live in pain of childbirth and parenting, strife in marriage, and toil in labor to make a living. Instead of reigning over the earth with dominion, they were consigned to slavery to Satan who rules to steal, kill, and destroy. Jesus said, "The thief comes only to steal and kill and destroy. I came that they may have life and have it abundantly" (John 10:10). In Genesis the consequences of Adam and Eve's sin is recorded, God declared:

"To the woman he said, 'I will surely multiply your pain in childbearing; in pain you shall bring forth children. Your desire shall be for your husband,
and he shall rule over you.' And to Adam he said, 'Because you have listened to the voice of your wife and have eaten of the tree of which I commanded you, 'You shall not eat of it,' cursed is the ground because of you; in pain you shall eat of it all the days of your life; thorns and thistles it shall bring forth for you; and you shall eat the plants of the field'" (Genesis 3:16-18).

Not only did Satan steal man's happiness on earth with spiritual death, but man was also cursed with physical death; for God declared that from dust we were created and to dust we will return.

"By the sweat of your face you shall eat bread, till you return to the ground, for out of it you were taken; for you are dust, and to dust you shall return" (Genesis 3:19).

Physical death in a state of spiritual separation from God on earth results in eternal separation from God forever. After death, we must face judgment before God and punishment for our sin, which is eternal destruction if we have not already restored our relationship with God.

"And just as it is appointed for man to die once, and after that comes judgment" (Hebrews 9:27).

"Then I saw a great white throne and him who was seated on it. From his presence earth and sky fled away, and no place was found for them. And I saw the dead, great and small, standing before the throne, and books were opened. Then another book was opened, which is the book of life. And the dead were judged by what was written in the books, according to what they had done. And the sea gave up the dead who were in it, Death and Hades gave up the dead who were in them, and they were judged, each one of them, according to what they had done. Then Death and Hades were thrown into the lake of fire. This is the second death, the lake of fire. And if anyone's name was not found written in the book of life, he was thrown into the lake of fire" (Revelation 20:11-15).

The worst part of eternal destruction in the lake of fire is that it is a place of permanent separation from God, away from His presence and glory of which we all enjoy many benefits while on this earth. Permanent separation from God is the ultimate consequence of Adam and Eve's sin and the result of each of us who choose to walk our own way without God.

"When the Lord Jesus is revealed from heaven with his mighty angels in flaming fire, inflicting vengeance on those who do not know God and on those who do not obey the gospel of our Lord Jesus. **They will suffer the punishment of eternal destruction, away from the**

presence of the Lord and from the glory of his might" (2 Thessalonians 1:7-9).

Cost to Redeem Life

God saw that there was no way we could save ourselves and no one to plead our case. The ransom or price of life was too costly. Our life costs more than what silver or gold could ever pay! So, God bought salvation with His own righteousness, which cost Him the precious blood of His son, Jesus. Jesus is the Mystery of God that redeems our lives.

"Truly no man can ransom another, or give to God the price of his life, for the ransom of their life is costly and can never suffice, that he should live on forever and never see the pit" (Psalm 49:7-9).

"He saw that there was no man, and wondered that there was no one to intercede; then his own arm brought him salvation, and his righteousness upheld him" (Isaiah 59:16).

"You were ransomed from the futile ways inherited from your forefathers, not with perishable things such as silver or gold, but with the precious blood of Christ, like that of a lamb without blemish or spot" (1 Peter 1:18-19).

CHAPTER 3 Questions for Thought and Discussion

1. Who defines what is "right" and what is "wrong"?

2. Do you believe that "all have sinned" (Romans 3:23)?

    Does that include you?

3. Why does God allow us to have free will which enables us to choose sin if we want?

4. a) What is justice?

   c) Should God overlook sin, why or why not? Does God overlook sin?

   c) Should God punish sin, why or why not? Does God punish sin?

5. In what ways do you 'go your own way,' 'do your own thing' or have your own way' instead of going God's way?

6. What do you believe happens after death?

   What does the Bible say happens without Christ after death?

CHAPTER 4

The Life of Jesus

So, who is this Jesus whom we have been talking about? Jesus is God. He was with Father God in the beginning before the world was created because He is God. Jesus created the world. He is called the Word of God because He came to earth in the form of a human man to communicate Father God to us in a human way that we could understand. He became flesh and dwelled among us so that we could see the glory of God in Him and come to know Father God through Him.

> "In the beginning was the Word, and the Word was with God, and the Word was God. He was in the beginning with God. All things were made through him, and without him was not anything made that was made. In him was life, and the life was the light of men. The light shines in the darkness, and the darkness has not overcome it...And the Word became flesh and dwelt among us, and we have seen his glory, glory as of the only Son from the Father, full of grace and truth" (John 1:1-5, 14).

During Jesus life on earth, He fulfilled several hundred prophesies written in the Old Testament. The Old Testament was written up to four thousand years before Jesus walked the earth. The probability that one human being could fulfill that many prophecies is impossible if He weren't God! Among prophesies that were written around 740-720 BC, there are two foretelling that the Savior would be born as a baby from the lineage of David by a virgin. The people of Israel were looking for this baby and all Jewish girls from the lineage of David wondered if they might be the mother of this special baby.

> "Therefore, the Lord himself will give you a sign. Behold, the virgin shall conceive and bear a son, and shall call his name Immanuel" (Isaiah 7:14).

> "For to us a child is born, to us a son is given;
> and the government shall be upon his shoulder,
> and his name shall be called Wonderful Counselor, Mighty God,
> Everlasting Father, Prince of Peace" (Isaiah 9:6).

Jesus' Birth Announced

Before Jesus was conceived, an angel appeared to a young Jewish girl named Mary who was engaged to be married to a man named Joseph to announce that she was to be the mother of the Savior of the world. Since she was a virgin, her pregnancy would only be possible because "the Holy Spirit came upon her, and the power of the Most High overshadowed her, so that the child to be born would be the Son of God." Later an angel appeared to Joseph in a dream to let him know that Mary was a virgin and that the baby in her was conceived by the power of the Holy Spirit of God, encouraging him that he should not hesitate to take her as his wife.

"In the sixth month the angel Gabriel was sent from God to a city of Galilee named Nazareth, to a virgin betrothed to a man whose name was Joseph, of the house of David. And the virgin's name was Mary. And he came to her and said, 'Greetings, O favored one, the Lord is with you!' But she was greatly troubled at the saying, and tried to discern what sort of greeting this might be. And the angel said to her, 'Do not be afraid, Mary, for you have found favor with God. And behold, you will conceive in your womb and bear a son, and you shall call his name Jesus. He will be great and will be called the Son of the Most High. And the Lord God will give to him the throne of his father David, and he will reign over the house of Jacob forever, and of his kingdom there will be no end.' And Mary said to the angel, 'How will this be, since I am a virgin?' And the angel answered her, 'The Holy Spirit will come upon you, and the power of the Most High will overshadow you; therefore, the child to be born will be called holy—the Son of God. And behold, your relative Elizabeth in her old age has also conceived a son, and this is the sixth month with her who was called barren. For nothing will be impossible with God.' And Mary said, 'Behold, I am the servant of the Lord; let it be to me according to your word.' And the angel departed from her" (Luke 1:26-38).

"Now the birth of Jesus Christ took place in this way. When his mother Mary had been betrothed to Joseph, before they came together, she was found to be with child from the Holy Spirit. And her husband Joseph, being a just man and unwilling to put her to shame, resolved to divorce her quietly. But as he considered these things, behold, an angel of the Lord appeared to him in a dream, saying, 'Joseph, son of David, do not fear to take Mary as your wife, for that which is conceived in her is from the Holy Spirit. She will bear a son, and you shall call his name Jesus, for he will save his people from their sins.' All this took place to fulfill what the Lord had spoken by the prophet: "Behold, the virgin shall conceive and bear a son, and they shall call his name Immanuel" (which means, God with us). When Joseph woke from sleep, he did as the angel of the Lord commanded him: he took his wife, but knew her not until she had given birth to a son. And he called his name Jesus" (Matthew 1:18-25).

Jesus' Birth

Jesus was born between the years 4- 6 BC. The entire calendar for the whole world is set around the birth of Jesus Christ! Before His birth, the dates are designated BC for "before Christ." After His birth, the dates are AD, which stands for "Anno Domini" which in Medieval Latin means "in the year of the Lord." Shortly before the baby was due to be born, Augustus, who was the Roman emperor, took a census that required every Israelite to register to be taxed in the city of their forefathers. This meant that Joseph and Mary had to travel from Nazareth to Bethlehem to be counted because they were of the lineage of King David. It happened that while they were in Bethlehem, Mary went into labor and gave birth to the baby Jesus, which had also been prophesied 700 hundred years earlier!

"But you, **O Bethlehem** Ephrathah, who are too little to be among the clans of Judah, from you shall come forth for me one who is to be ruler in Israel,
whose coming forth is from of old, from ancient days." (Micah 5:2 ca. 700 BC).

The night that Mary went into labor, the city was so full of people registering for the census that there was no room for them in the inns. Without a place to deliver, Mary gave birth to Jesus in a stable that was for the animals behind the inn. Angels announced Jesus' birth to shepherds tending their sheep in a nearby field. The shepherds eagerly came to see the newborn baby who was announced by angels to be Savior, Messiah, and Lord. After seeing the baby, the shepherds returned to their flocks telling everyone they met and glorifying God for all they had heard and seen.

"In those days a decree went out from Caesar Augustus that all the world should be registered. This was the first registration when Quirinius was governor of Syria. And all went to be registered, each to

his own town. And Joseph also went up from Galilee, from the town of Nazareth, to Judea, to the city of David, which is called Bethlehem, because he was of the house and lineage of David, to be registered with Mary, his betrothed, who was with child. And while they were there, the time came for her to give birth. And she gave birth to her firstborn son and wrapped him in swaddling clothes and laid him in a manger, because there was no place for them in the inn.
And in the same region there were shepherds out in the field, keeping watch over their flock by night. And an angel of the Lord appeared to them, and the glory of the Lord shone around them, and they were filled with great fear. And the angel said to them, 'Fear not, for behold, I bring you good news of great joy that will be for all the people. For unto you is born this day in the city of David a Savior, who is Christ the Lord. And this will be a sign for you: you will find a baby wrapped in swaddling clothes and lying in a manger.' And suddenly there was with the angel a multitude of the heavenly host praising God and saying, 'Glory to God in the highest, and on earth peace among those with whom he is pleased!' When the angels went away from them into heaven, the shepherds said to one another, 'Let us go over to Bethlehem and see this thing that has happened, which the Lord has made known to us.' And they went with haste and found Mary and Joseph, and the baby lying in a manger. And when they saw it, they made known the saying that had been told them concerning this child. And all who heard it wondered at what the shepherds told them. But Mary treasured up all these things, pondering them in her heart. And the shepherds returned, glorifying and praising God for all they had heard and seen, as it had been told them" (Luke 2:1-20).

Matthew 2 tells us that around that time, astronomers, traditionally called "wise men," traveled from countries east of Bethlehem possibly Persia, following a star which they interpreted as the announcement of the birth of a great King. When the star rested over the house where Jesus was, they entered bearing expensive gifts of gold, frankincense, and myrrh. These gifts were to be God's provision for the baby as the new family was warned in a dream to escape to Egypt before King Herod began to search for baby Jesus to kill Him. Years later, after Herod had died, Joseph was told in a dream that it was safe for the family to leave Egypt and return to Nazareth. We only have one story of Jesus' childhood where, at age 12, He was teaching the teachers of the temple in Jerusalem. After that the Scriptures pick up with the beginning of Jesus' ministry at age 30.

Jesus' Ministry

Jesus' ministry involved travelling all over Galilee proclaiming that "the Kingdom of God was at hand," which meant that Jesus, the King and Lord, was now present on earth to reign and enforce His sovereignty and dominion. This was a clear declaration by Jesus to Satan that He had come to take back dominion of the earth. "The reason the Son of God appeared was to destroy the works of the devil" (1 John 3:8). Jesus proved that He is the Son of God and that He has power over Satan by doing miracles and healing many sick people. He also taught large crowds in the temple, from village to village, and on the countryside. Jesus often used stories called 'parables' that illustrated 'the Kingdom of God' with common things the people were acquainted with like farming. The Gospels: Matthew, Mark, Luke, and John, are full of Jesus' teaching, parables, and accounts of the miracles he did.

> "And he went throughout all Galilee, teaching in their synagogues and proclaiming the gospel of the kingdom and healing every disease and every affliction among the people. So, his fame spread throughout all Syria, and they brought him all the sick, those afflicted with various diseases and pains, those oppressed by demons, epileptics, and paralytics, and he healed them. And great crowds followed him from Galilee and the Decapolis, and from Jerusalem and Judea, and from beyond the Jordan" (Matthew 4:23-25).

> "And Jesus went throughout all the cities and villages, teaching in their synagogues and proclaiming the gospel of the kingdom and healing every disease and every affliction. When he saw the crowds, he had compassion for them, because they were harassed and helpless, like sheep without a shepherd" (Matthew 9:34-35).

Towards the end of His three-year ministry, Jesus confronted the spiritual leaders of the people with their hypocrisy and lack of knowledge of the things of God. This resulted in the spiritual leaders of Israel plotting to take His life.

Jesus' Trial

During the week of Passover, the spiritual leaders of Israel had Jesus arrested and brought Him before Pilot for trial to be sentenced to death. Pilot saw nothing worthy of the death sentence and tried to avoid sentencing Jesus to death by sending Him to Herod. When Herod sent Him back, Pilot had Jesus scourged and presented Him to the people in hopes that this would appease the people. The people, however, cried out all the more for Jesus to be crucified and the religious leaders continued to demand His execution. Pilot gave into the pressure and sentenced Jesus to death on a cross.

> "Then the whole company of them arose and brought him before Pilate. And they began to accuse him, saying, 'We found this man misleading our nation and forbidding us to give tribute to Caesar, and saying that he himself is Christ, a king.' And Pilate asked him, 'Are you the King of the Jews?' And he answered him, 'You have said so.' Then Pilate said to the chief priests and the crowds, 'I find no guilt in this man.' But they were urgent, saying, 'He stirs up the people, teaching throughout all Judea, from Galilee even to this place.' When Pilate heard this, he asked whether the man was a Galilean. And when he learned that he belonged to Herod's jurisdiction, he sent him over to Herod, who was himself in Jerusalem at that time. When Herod saw Jesus, he was very glad, for he had long desired to see him, because he had heard about him, and he was hoping to see some sign done by him. So, he questioned him at some length, but he made no answer. The chief priests and the scribes stood by, vehemently accusing him. And Herod with his soldiers treated him with contempt and mocked him. Then, arraying him in splendid clothing, he sent him back to Pilate. And Herod and Pilate became friends with each other that very day, for before this they had been at enmity with each other. Pilate then called together the chief priests and the rulers and the people, and said to them, 'You brought me this man as one who was misleading the people. And after examining him before you, behold, I did not find this man guilty of any of your charges against him. Neither did Herod, for he sent him back to us. Look, nothing deserving death has been done by him. I will therefore punish and release him.' But they all cried out together, 'Away with this man, and release to us Barabbas'— a man who had been thrown into prison for an insurrection started in the city and for murder. Pilate addressed them once more, desiring to release Jesus, but they kept shouting, 'Crucify, crucify him!' A third time he said to them, 'Why, what evil has he done? I have found in him no guilt deserving death. I will therefore punish and release him.' But they were urgent, demanding with loud cries that he should be crucified. And their voices prevailed. So, Pilate decided that their demand should be granted" (Luke 23:1-24).

"So, when Pilate saw that he was gaining nothing, but rather that a riot was beginning, he took water and washed his hands before the crowd, saying, 'I am innocent of this man's blood; see to it yourselves.' And all the people answered, 'His blood be on us and on our children!' Then he released for them Barabbas, and **having scourged Jesus**, delivered him to be crucified. Then the soldiers of the governor took Jesus into the governor's headquarters, and they gathered the whole battalion before him. And they stripped him and put a scarlet robe on him, and twisting together a crown of thorns, they put it on his head and put a reed in his right hand. And kneeling before him, they mocked him, saying, 'Hail, King of the Jews!' And they spit on him and took the reed and struck him on the head. And when they had mocked him, they stripped him of the robe and put his own clothes on him and led him away to crucify him" (Matthew 27:24-31).

Jesus' Scourge

Before Jesus was crucified, He endured being scourged which was required by Roman law before an execution or as a punishment for a dangerous crime or crime against the state. Jewish law limited the flogging to 39 lashes, but it is impossible to know whether the Roman guards obeyed that Jewish law because they were allowed to torment the victims at will. Scourging or flogging was the most painful form of torture the Romans could think of. It was reserved for the most dangerous criminals, non-Roman, and low-caste slaves. It was humiliating for Jesus as He was stripped of all of His clothes and tied to a whipping post where His back, buttocks, and tops of His legs were exposed in public. The whip that was used had several leather thongs in which were tied small pieces of metal or pieces of sheep bones. When the victim was whipped, these small pieces of metal and bone would embed in the skin and eventually muscle tissue, tearing away the tissue with every blow, layer-by-layer, causing considerable blood loss. It is likely that the reason Jesus was unable to carry His cross was because the muscles in the back of His thighs had been completely ripped off the bone so He was no longer able to walk. Scourging may also have been the reason Jesus died after only six hours on the cross. His death was quicker than most crucifixions, which were intended to be a slow, painful method of death lasting for several days. As described in the above passage, during the scourging it was common for the guards who were doing the torture to humiliate, taunt and torment the victim.

"I gave my back to those who strike, and my cheeks to those who pull out the beard; I hid not my face from disgrace and spitting" (Isaiah 50:6, written ca. 740-720 BC).

At about 8:00 in the morning, Jesus began to walk the 650 yards from Pilot's Praetorian to Golgotha called Via Dolorosa or the "way of suffering" where He was to be crucified. Due to His physical condition, He could not carry the crossbar of His cross, which weighed around 100 pounds. Therefore, the guards forced a man from the crowd named Simon to carry the crossbar for Him. According to Mark 15:25 He was hung on the cross around 9 a.m. Jesus was crucified with two other criminals. While He hung on the cross, many people including guards, religious leaders, onlookers, and even one of the criminals who was crucified at His side, jeered at and taunted Him.

"As they went out, they found a man of Cyrene, Simon by name. They compelled this man to carry his cross. And when they came to a place called Golgotha (which means Place of a Skull), they offered him wine to drink, mixed with gall, but when he tasted it, he would not drink it. And when they had crucified him, they divided his garments among them by casting lots. Then they sat down and kept watch over him there. And over his head they put the charge against him, which read, 'This is Jesus, the King of the Jews.' Then two robbers were crucified with him, one on the right and one on the left. **And those who passed by derided him, wagging their heads** and saying, 'You who would destroy the temple and rebuild it in three days, save yourself! If you are the Son of God, come down from the cross.' **So also, the chief priests, with the scribes and elders, mocked him**, saying, 'He saved others; he cannot save himself. He is the King of Israel; let him come down now from the cross, and we will believe in him. He trusts in God; let God deliver him now, if he desires him. For he said, 'I am the Son of God.' **And the robbers who were crucified with him also reviled him in the same way**" (Matthew 27:32-44).

The Crucifixion

The Romans used crucifixion for non-Roman citizens, slaves, the vilest criminals, and those who had committed treason. Crucifixion is where we get the word "excruciate," which means to cause great suffering and torment. Death by crucifixion was perfected by Rome to inflict the most agony and pain on the victim.

It caused a slow death, sometimes lasting a week or more, with insects and birds preying on the victims as they hung on a cross, exposed to the elements. As the victim hung on the cross naked for days on end, the soldiers and crowds would harass and torment them.

Jesus would have been secured to a cross of wood by extending His arms out along the crossbar with nails that were 7" long and 3/8" wide being hammered through the bones and ligaments of His wrists and His feet causing severe nerve damage and bleeding. The cross was then stood upright so that the nails in His hands and feet bore Jesus' entire weight causing excruciating pain. The extension of Jesus' arms would likely have inhibited His ability to inhale and exhale freely. There is evidence that some victims were given a small piece of wood nailed to the cross for them to lean against to support their weight so that they were better able to inhale and exhale, but we don't know whether Jesus was given one or not. Death by crucifixion could be attributed to one or more of several medical crises: shock, suffocation because of inability to inhale or exhale, cardiac and respiratory arrest, bleeding to death, exhaustion, or dehydration. In Jesus' case, since He was only on the cross for 6 hours instead of the 6 days it often took, He could have suffered cardiac or respiratory failure.

> "I am poured out like water, and all my bones are out of joint; my heart is like wax; it is melted within my breast; my strength is dried up like a potsherd, and my tongue sticks to my jaws; you lay me in the dust of death. For dogs encompass me; a company of evildoers encircles me; they have pierced my hands and feet—I can count all my bones— they stare and gloat over me; they divide my garments among them, and for my clothing they cast lots" (Psalm 22:13-18 written ca.1000BC).

> "As many were astonished at you— his appearance was so marred, beyond human semblance, and his form beyond that of the children of mankind—...He was despised and rejected by men; a man of sorrows, and acquainted with grief; and as one from whom men hide their faces he was despised, and we esteemed him not. Surely, he has borne our griefs and carried our sorrows; yet we esteemed him stricken, smitten by God, and afflicted. But he was pierced for our transgressions; he was crushed for our iniquities;
> upon him was the chastisement that brought us peace, and with his wounds we are healed. All we like sheep have gone astray; we have turned—every one—to his own way; and the LORD has laid on him the iniquity of us all.
> He was oppressed, and he was afflicted, yet he opened not his mouth;

like a lamb that is led to the slaughter, and like a sheep that before its shearers is silent, so he opened not his mouth" (Isaiah 52:13, 53:3-7 written ca. 740-720 BC).

Seven Words of Jesus

Jesus spoke seven words from the cross, which are recorded in the four gospels and are highlighted in the following passages.

"And Jesus said, **'Father, forgive them, for they know not what they do.'** And they cast lots to divide his garments. And the people stood by, watching, but the rulers scoffed at him, saying, 'He saved others; let him save himself, if he is the Christ of God, his Chosen One!' The soldiers also mocked him, coming up and offering him sour wine and saying, 'If you are the King of the Jews, save yourself!' There was also an inscription over him, 'This is the King of the Jews.' One of the criminals who were hanged railed at him, saying, **'Are you not the Christ? Save yourself and us!'** But the other rebuked him, saying, 'Do you not fear God, since you are under the same sentence of condemnation? And we indeed justly, for we are receiving the due reward of our deeds; but this man has done nothing wrong.' And he said, 'Jesus, remember me when you come into your kingdom.' And he said to him, **'Truly, I say to you, today you will be with me in Paradise'"** (Luke 23:32-43).

"Now from the sixth hour there was darkness over all the land until the ninth hour. And about the ninth hour Jesus cried out with a loud voice, saying, 'Eli, Eli, lema sabachthani?' that is, **'My God, my God, why have you forsaken me?' And some of the bystanders, hearing it, said,** 'This man is calling Elijah.' And one of them at once ran and took a sponge, filled it with sour wine, and put it on a reed and gave it to him to drink. But the others said, 'Wait, let us see whether Elijah will come to save him.' And Jesus cried out again with a loud voice and yielded up his spirit. And behold, the curtain of the temple was torn in two, from top to bottom. And the earth shook, and the rocks were split. The tombs also were opened. And many bodies of the saints who had fallen asleep were raised, and coming out of the tombs after his resurrection they went into the holy city and appeared to many. When the centurion and those who were with him, keeping watch over Jesus, saw the earthquake and what took place, they were filled with awe and said, 'Truly this was the Son of God!' There were also many women there, looking on from a distance, who had followed Jesus from Galilee, ministering to him, among whom were Mary Magdalene and Mary the mother of James and Joseph and the mother of the sons of Zebedee" (Matthew 27:45-55).

"It was now about the sixth hour, and there was darkness over the whole land until the ninth hour, while the sun's light failed. And the curtain of the temple was torn in two. Then Jesus, calling out with a loud voice, said, 'Father, into your **hands I commit my spirit!**' And having said this he breathed his last. Now when the centurion saw what had taken place, he praised God, saying, 'Certainly this man was innocent!' And all the crowds that had assembled for this spectacle, when they saw what had taken place, returned home beating their breasts. And all his acquaintances and the women who had followed him from Galilee stood at a distance watching these things" (Luke 23:44-49).

"So, the soldiers did these things, but standing by the cross of Jesus were his mother and his mother's sister, Mary the wife of Clopas, and Mary Magdalene. When Jesus saw his mother and the disciple whom he loved standing nearby, he said to his mother, 'Woman, behold, your son!' Then he said to the disciple, **'Behold, your mother!'** And from that hour the disciple took her to his own home. After this, Jesus, knowing that all was now finished, said (to fulfill the Scripture), **'I thirst.'** A jar full of sour wine stood there, so they put a sponge full of the sour wine on a hyssop branch and held it to his mouth. When Jesus had received the sour wine, he said, **'It is finished,'** and he bowed his head and gave up his spirit" (John 19:25-30).

Jesus' Death

Jesus died around 3:00 in the afternoon. By that time, eerily it had already been pitch-dark since noon. Upon His death, the curtain of the temple which separated the people from the Holy Place of God's presence, was torn in two from top to bottom—opening the way to fellowship with God. The earth shook, rocks split, and tombs were opened! Many bodies of the saints were raised from the dead and seen coming out of their tombs. Because of the supernatural phenomena surrounding His death, many bystanders became convinced that Jesus really was the Son of God.

Jesus' Burial

According to Jewish law, it was important to get Jesus down from the cross the day He died because the following day was the Sabbath. To be sure He was dead, the soldiers pierced a spear from His side into His heart rather than the customary breaking of His leg. The fact that "blood and water" flowed from His side, strongly suggests that the spear punctured the sac surrounding the heart which had filled with water and then pierced the heart which was full of blood. Being pierced with a spear, fulfilled another Old Testament Scripture, Psalm 34:20, which says that none of His bones were broken.

There were many witnesses to Jesus' death: the centurion, the crowd, His disciples, and the women who followed Him. There were also the people involved in His burial: Joseph of Arimathea, who was a respected Jewish leader of the Jewish Sanhedrin, gave Jesus his own tomb, Nicodemus, a ruler of the Jews, brought burial spices, and Mary Magdalene and the other Mary "saw the tomb and how his body was laid" (Luke 23:55).

> "When it was evening, there came a rich man from Arimathea, named **Joseph**, who also was a disciple of Jesus. He went to Pilate and asked for the body of Jesus. Then Pilate ordered it to be given to him. And Joseph took the body and wrapped it in a clean linen shroud and laid it in his own new tomb, which he had cut in the rock. And he rolled a great stone to the entrance of the tomb and went away. **Mary Magdalene** and **the other Mary** were there, sitting opposite the tomb" (Matthew 27:57-61).

> "Since it was the day of Preparation, and so that the bodies would not remain on the cross on the Sabbath (for that Sabbath was a high day), the Jews asked Pilate that their legs might be broken and that they might be taken away. So, the soldiers came and broke the legs of the first, and of the other who had been crucified with him. But when they came to Jesus and saw that he was already dead, they did not break his legs. But one of the **soldiers pierced his side with a spear, and at once there came out blood and water**. He who saw it has borne witness—his testimony is true, and he knows that he is telling the truth—that you also may believe. For these things took place that the Scripture might be fulfilled: 'Not one of his bones will be broken.' And

again, another Scripture says, "They will look on him whom they have pierced." After these things **Joseph of Arimathea**, who was a disciple of Jesus, but secretly for fear of the Jews, asked Pilate that he might take away the body of Jesus, and Pilate gave him permission. So, he came and took away his body. **Nicodemus** also, who earlier had come to Jesus by night, came bringing a mixture of myrrh and aloes, about seventy-five pounds in weight. So, they took the body of Jesus and bound it in linen cloths with the spices, as is the burial custom of the Jews. Now in the place where he was crucified there was a garden, and in the garden a new tomb in which no one had yet been laid. So, because of the Jewish day of Preparation, since the tomb was close at hand, they laid Jesus there" (John 19:31-42).

The Jewish leaders remembered that Jesus had prophesied that He would rise from the dead in three days (see Matthew 16:21; 17:23; 20:19). They were worried that somehow His body would end up missing, which would prove a bigger problem for them, so they asked Pilot to secure the grave. Pilot gave permission to secure the grave in three ways: there was a huge stone rolled in front of the entrance to the tomb (see Mark 16:4), there was Pilot's Roman seal which sealed the stone in place, and there was a Roman guard watching over it. A Roman guard was typically made of a minimum of 16 men who were spaced six square feet apart, and who were not allowed to sit or lean but must stand at attention. In the event that one of the guards fell asleep, the Roman punishment was that the entire guard would be beaten and burned in their own clothes.

The next day, that is, after the day of Preparation, the chief priests and the Pharisees gathered before Pilate and said, "Sir, we remember how that impostor said, while he was still alive, 'After three days I will rise.' Therefore, order the tomb to be made secure until the third day, lest his disciples go and steal him away and tell the people, 'He has risen from the dead,' and the last fraud will be worse than the first." Pilate said to them, "You have a guard of soldiers. Go, **make it as secure as you can.**" So, **they went and made the tomb secure by sealing the stone and setting a guard** (Matthew 27:62-66).

Jesus' Resurrection

The day after the Sabbath, the women prepared the burial spices and left early in the morning to embalm Jesus properly, since they did not have time to do so before because of the Sabbath. As the women approached the tomb, they wondered how they would get into the tomb since a huge stone had been rolled in front of the tomb. To their surprise, when they got to the tomb the stone had been rolled away, and the guard was nowhere to be found. Jesus was not in the tomb, but instead an angel was there announcing, "He is not here, for He has risen", and that He would meet them and the disciples in Galilee. The women ran and told the disciples, two of which ran to the tomb to see for themselves and found the tomb exactly how the women had told them—Jesus' body gone, with only His burial clothes left in His place.

"Now after the Sabbath, toward the dawn of the first day of the week, Mary Magdalene and the other Mary went to see the tomb. And behold, there was a great earthquake, for an **angel of the Lord** descended from heaven and came and **rolled back the stone** and sat on it. His appearance was like lightning, and his clothing white as snow. And for fear of him **the guards trembled and became like dead men**. But the angel said to the women, '"Do not be afraid, for I know that you seek Jesus who was crucified. **He is not here, for he has risen, as he said. Come, see the place where he lay**. Then go quickly and tell his disciples that he has risen from the dead, and behold, **he is going before you to Galilee; there you will see him**. See, I have told you.' So, they departed quickly from the tomb with fear and great joy, and ran to tell his disciples. And behold, Jesus met them and said, 'Greetings!' And they came up and took hold of his feet and worshiped him. Then Jesus said to them, 'Do not be afraid; go and tell my brothers to go to Galilee, and there they will see me'" (Matthew 28:1-10).

"When the Sabbath was past, Mary Magdalene, Mary the mother of James, and Salome bought spices, so that they might go and anoint him. And very early on the first day of the week, when the sun had risen, they went to the tomb. And they were saying to one another, 'Who will roll away the stone for us from the entrance of the tomb?' And looking up, they saw that **the stone had been rolled back—it was very large**. And entering the tomb, they saw a **young man sitting on the right side, dressed in a white robe**, and they were alarmed. And he said to them, "Do not be alarmed. You seek Jesus of Nazareth, who was crucified. **He has risen; he is not here**. See the place where they laid him. But go, tell his disciples and Peter **that he is going before you to Galilee**. There you will see him, just as he told you." And they went out and fled from the tomb, for trembling and astonishment had seized them, and they said nothing to anyone, for they were afraid" (Mark 16:1-8).

"But on the first day of the week, at early dawn, they went to the tomb, taking the spices, they had prepared. And they found the **stone rolled away from the tomb**, but when they went in, they **did not find the body of the Lord Jesus**. While they were perplexed about this, behold, **two men stood by them in dazzling apparel**. And as they were frightened and bowed their faces to the ground, the men said to them, "Why do you seek the living among the dead? He is not here, but has risen. Remember **how he told you**, while he was still in Galilee, that the Son of Man must be delivered into the hands of sinful men and be crucified and on the third day rise." And they remembered his words, and returning from the tomb they told all these things to the eleven and to all the rest. Now it was Mary Magdalene and Joanna and Mary the mother of James and the other women with them who told these things to the apostles, but these words seemed to them an idle tale, and they did not believe them. But Peter rose and ran to the tomb; stooping and looking in, he **saw the linen cloths by themselves**; and he went home marveling at what had happened" (Luke 24:1-12).

"Now on the first day of the week Mary Magdalene came to the tomb early, while it was still dark, and saw that the **stone had been taken away from the tomb**. So, she ran and went to Simon Peter and the other disciple, the one whom Jesus loved, and said to them, 'They have taken the Lord out of the tomb, and we do not know where they have laid him.' So, Peter went out with the other disciple, and they were going toward the tomb. Both of them were running together, but the other disciple outran Peter and reached the tomb first. And stooping to look in, he **saw the linen cloths lying there**, but he did not go in. Then Simon Peter came, following him, and went into the tomb. He saw the linen cloths lying there, and the face cloth, which had been on Jesus' head, not lying with the **linen cloths but folded up in a place by itself**. Then the other disciple, who had reached the tomb first, also went in, and he saw and believed; for as yet they did not understand the Scripture, that he must rise from the dead. Then the disciples went back to their homes" (John 20:1-10).

Appearances

Jesus' resurrection is truly remarkable. Throughout history, the one thing that is an undisputed fact is that after someone dies, they are dead and do not return to life. Jesus' resurrection is an incredible miracle that proves He is God! After Jesus' resurrection, to the amazement and surprise of everyone, He appeared to many people beginning with Mary Magdalene in the garden near the tomb. Next, He joined two men, one of whom was named Cleopas, who were walking down the road. After that He appeared to His disciples while they were hiding behind locked doors at a time when Thomas the Apostle was not there. Later He appeared again to the disciples when Thomas was there. In John 21, He appeared to the disciples while they were fishing and He had a conversation with Peter that is recorded there. In general, according to 1 Corinthians 15, He appeared to over 500 people after His resurrection, before His ascension. After His ascension, He appeared to the Apostle Paul.

Jesus appears to Mary Magdalene and Two Men on the Road

"Now when he rose early on the first day of the week, he appeared first to Mary Magdalene, from whom he had cast out seven demons. She went and told those who had been with him, as they mourned and wept. But when they heard that he was alive and had been seen by her, they would not believe it. After these things he appeared in another form to two of them, as they were walking into the country. And they went back and told the rest, but they did not believe them" (Mark 16:9-13).

Jesus Appears to Mary Magdalene

"But Mary stood weeping outside the tomb, and as she wept, she stooped to look into the tomb. And she saw two angels in white, sitting where the body of Jesus had lain, one at the head and one at the feet. They said to her, 'Woman, why are you weeping?' She said to them, 'They have taken away my Lord, and I do not know where they have laid him.' Having said this, she turned around and saw Jesus standing, but she did not know that it was Jesus. Jesus said to her, 'Woman, why are you weeping? Whom are you seeking?' Supposing him to be the gardener, she said to him, 'Sir, if you have carried him away, tell me where you have laid him, and I will take him away.' Jesus said to her, 'Mary.' She turned and said to him in Aramaic, 'Rabboni!' (which means Teacher). Jesus said to her, 'Do not cling to me, for I have not yet ascended to the Father; but go to my brothers and say to them, 'I am ascending to my Father and your Father, to my God and your God." Mary Magdalene went and announced to the disciples, 'I have seen the Lord'—and that he had said these things to her" (John 20:11-18).

Jesus Appears to the Disciples
"On the evening of that day, the first day of the week, the doors being locked where the disciples were for fear of the Jews, Jesus came and stood among them and said to them, 'Peace be with you.' When he had said this, he showed them his hands and his side. Then the disciples were glad when they saw the Lord. Jesus said to them again, 'Peace be with you. As the Father has sent me, even so I am sending you.' And when he had said this, he breathed on them and said to them, 'Receive the Holy Spirit. If you forgive the sins of any, they are forgiven them; if you withhold forgiveness from any, it is withheld'" (John 20:19-23) (cf. Luke 24:13-35).

Jesus Appears to Thomas
"Now Thomas, one of the Twelve, called the Twin, was not with them when Jesus came. So, the other disciples told him, 'We have seen the Lord.' But he said to them, 'Unless I see in his hands the mark of the nails, and place my finger into the mark of the nails, and place my hand into his side, I will never believe.' Eight days later, his disciples were inside again, and Thomas was with them. Although the doors were locked, Jesus came and stood among them and said, 'Peace be with you.' Then he said to Thomas, 'Put your finger here, and see my hands; and put out your hand, and place it in my side. Do not disbelieve, but believe.' Thomas answered him, 'My Lord and my God!' Jesus said to him, 'Have you believed because you have seen me? Blessed are those who have not seen and yet have believed'" (John 20:24-29).

Jesus Appears to 500
"For I delivered to you as of first importance what I also received: that Christ died for our sins in accordance with the Scriptures, that he was buried, that he was raised on the third day in accordance with the Scriptures, and that he appeared to Cephas, then to the twelve. **Then he appeared to more than five hundred brothers at one time,** most of whom are still alive, though some have fallen asleep. Then he appeared to James, then to all the apostles. Last of all, as to one untimely born, he appeared also to me" (1 Corinthians 15:2-8).

Evidence of Jesus Death and Resurrection

In summary, there is much evidence that Jesus died and rose from the dead, as we have already covered.

1.   Jesus' Prophecy about Himself

Jesus Himself prophesied that He would die and then rise from the dead on the third day.

> "The Son of Man must suffer many things and be rejected by the elders and chief priests and scribes, and be killed, and on the third day be raised" (Luke 9:22).

> "And taking the twelve, he said to them, 'See, we are going up to Jerusalem, and everything that is written about the Son of Man by the prophets will be accomplished. For he will be delivered over to the Gentiles and will be mocked and shamefully treated and spit upon. And after flogging him, they will kill him, and on the third day he will rise'" (Luke 18:31-33).

2.   Jesus' Death and Burial

The crowd that was present at Jesus' resurrection attested of Jesus death (see Luke 23:48-49). Two Jewish leaders, Joseph of Arimathea, and Nicodemus took responsibility for His burial, while the women who followed Jesus saw the tomb and where He was laid. The centurion who was responsible for Jesus' death testified to Pilate that Jesus had indeed died. There is also the testimony of the Jewish leaders in Matthew 27:62-66 who went to Pilate and asked for Jesus' grave to be secured because they feared the prophesy of His resurrection and in Matthew 28:11-15 it was the Chief Priests that paid the guard to lie about the Jesus' resurrection by saying that His disciples had stolen the body.

> "After these things **Joseph of Arimathea**, who was a disciple of Jesus, but secretly for fear of the Jews, asked Pilate that he might take away the body of Jesus, and Pilate gave him permission. So, he came and took away his body. **Nicodemus** also, who earlier had come to Jesus

by night, came bringing a mixture of myrrh and aloes, about seventy-five pounds in weight" (John 19:38-39).

"And when the **centurion**, who stood facing him, saw that in this way he breathed his last, he said, "Truly this man was the Son of God!" There were also **women** looking on from a distance, among whom were Mary Magdalene, and Mary the mother of James the younger and of Joses, and Salome....Joseph of Arimathea, a respected member of the council, who was also himself looking for the kingdom of God, took courage and went to Pilate and asked for the body of Jesus. **Pilate was surprised to hear that he should have already died. And summoning the centurion, he asked him whether he was already dead. And when he learned from the centurion that he was dead, he granted the corpse to Joseph**" (Mark 15:39-40, 43-45).

3. **The empty tomb**

The empty tomb is the biggest evidence that Jesus has risen from the dead. All three things that the Romans did to secure the tomb were undone: the stone was rolled away by an earthquake, the seal was consequently broken, the guards fell back as dead men, and an angel was there declaring that "Jesus is not here, He is risen." All that remained was the burial cloth which proved He had been there, but now He was gone.

4. **Eyewitness appearances**

As we saw, there were personal face-to-face encounters with Jesus by the women who followed Him, by His disciples, and by over 500 other followers including the 120 that were waiting for the Baptism of the Holy Spirit at Pentecost as sited by Peter.

"This Jesus God raised up, and of that **we all are witnesses**" (Acts 2:32).

"Then **he appeared to more than five hundred brothers at one time**" (1 Corinthians 15:6).

5. **Followers of Christ**

One evidence that we have not talked about was that these disciples, who all fled at Jesus' death and were found hiding behind locked doors after His death for fear of their lives, had a dramatic change of heart and became bold witnesses for Jesus Christ after His resurrection. Many of the disciples and followers of Jesus were tortured and martyred for their faith in and proclamation of the death and resurrection of Jesus. The fact that His followers were not dissuaded by their persecution but continued to proclaim Jesus' death and resurrection is a testimony that reaches us today.

"Now if Christ is proclaimed as raised from the dead, how can some of you say that there is no resurrection of the dead? But if there is no resurrection of the dead, then not even Christ has been raised. And if Christ has not been raised, then our preaching is in vain and your faith is in vain. We are even found to be misrepresenting God, because we testified about God that he raised Christ, whom he did not raise if it is true that the dead are not raised. For if the dead are not raised, not even Christ has been raised. And if Christ has not been raised, your faith is futile and you are still in your sins. Then those also who have fallen asleep in Christ have perished. If in Christ we have hope in this life only, we are of all people most to be pitied. **But in fact, Christ has been raised from the dead**, the first fruits of those who have fallen asleep. For as by a man came death, by a man has come also the resurrection of the dead. For as in Adam all die, so also in Christ shall all be made alive" (1 Corinthians 15:12-22).

6. **Historical Accounts**

"Men of Israel, listen to these words: Jesus the Nazarene, a man attested to you by God with miracles and wonders and signs which God performed through Him in your midst, just as you yourselves know-- this [Man,] delivered over by the predetermined plan and foreknowledge of God, you nailed to a cross by the hands of godless men and put [Him] to death. "But God raised Him up again, putting an end to the agony of death, since it was impossible for Him to be held in its power" (Acts 2:22-24).

The first record of Jesus' death and resurrection was that of the Apostle Peter in Acts 2:22-24. The Apostle Paul also testified of Jesus resurrection from the dead in 1 Corinthians 15 and in the rest of the New Testament.

Although there is not much recorded history for this time period of the world outside of Scripture, there were two historians who spoke of Jesus' death, resurrection, and the disciples persistent witness of it.

> "Christus, from whom the name had its origin, suffered the extreme penalty during the reign of Tiberius at the hands of one of our procurators, Pontius Pilatus, and a most mischievous superstition, thus checked for the moment, again broke out not only in Judaea, the first source of the evil, but even in Rome." *Tacitus (AD55-120) Roman historian: (Annals, XV, 44).*

> "Now there was about this time Jesus, a wise man, if it be lawful to call him a man, for he was a doer of wonderful works, a teacher of such men as receive the truth with pleasure. He drew over to him both many of the Jews and many of the Gentiles. He was the Christ, and when Pilate, at the suggestion of the principal men among us, had condemned him to the cross, those that loved him at the first did not forsake him; for he appeared to them alive again the third day; as the divine prophets had foretold these and ten thousand other wonderful things concerning him. And the tribe of Christians so named from him are not extinct at this day." *Josephus ben Mattathias, (37-100AD) Jewish priest, general and historian, (Jewish Antiquities, XVIII, 33)*

7. **Early believers and Church History**

The final evidence is the testimony of the early church. The early believers and apostolic fathers believed in Jesus' resurrection so much that they made Jesus' resurrection their first Christian celebration. The earliest church councils and writings all support Jesus' resurrection as central and essential to Christianity.

The Apostle's Creed (3rd-4th centuries A.D.)
"I believe ...in Jesus Christ his only son our Lord; who was conceived by the Holy Spirit, born of the virgin Mary; **suffered under Pontius Pilate, was crucified, dead and buried; the third day he rose from the dead**; he ascended into heaven; and sitteth at the right hand of God the Father Almighty, from thence he shall come to judge the quick and the dead."

The Nicene Creed (A.D. 325; revised at Constantinople A.D. 381)
"I believe…in one Lord Jesus Christ,…who for us men and for our salvation, came down from heaven, and was incarnate by the Holy Spirit of the Virgin Mary, and was made man; and **was crucified also for us under Pontius Pilate; he suffered and was buried; and the third day he rose again**, according to the Scriptures; and ascended into heaven, and sitteth on the right hand of the Father; and he shall come again, with glory, to judge both the quick and the dead; whose kingdom shall have no end."

Jesus' Ascension

Finally, forty days after Jesus' resurrection He ascended up into the clouds of heaven while His disciples watched from below, staring off into the sky until two angels appeared. The angels told the disciples that Jesus had been taken up into heaven and someday would return, descending to earth in the same way He ascended into the clouds. Until then, He sits at the right hand of God the Father with all power and authority over the earth.

> "Then he led them out as far as Bethany, and lifting up his hands he blessed them. **While he blessed them, he parted from them and was carried up into heaven**. And they worshiped him and returned to Jerusalem with great joy, and were continually in the temple blessing God" (Luke 24:50-53).

> "In the first book, O Theophilus, I have dealt with all that Jesus began to do and teach, until the day when he was taken up, after he had given commands through the Holy Spirit to the apostles whom he had chosen. He presented himself alive to them after his suffering by many proofs, appearing to them during forty days and speaking about the kingdom of God. And while staying with them he ordered them not to depart from Jerusalem, but to wait for the promise of the Father, which, he said, 'you heard from me; for John baptized with water, but you will be baptized with the Holy Spirit not many days from now.' So, when they had come together, they asked him, 'Lord, will you at this time restore the kingdom to Israel?' He said to them, 'It is not for you to know times or seasons that the Father has fixed by his own authority. But you will receive power when the Holy Spirit has come upon you, and you will be my witnesses in Jerusalem and in all Judea

and Samaria, and to the end of the earth.' **And when he had said these things, as they were looking on, he was lifted up, and a cloud took him out of their sight. And while they were gazing into heaven as he went, behold, two men stood by them in white robes, and said, "Men of Galilee, why do you stand looking into heaven? This Jesus, who was taken up from you into heaven, will come in the same way as you saw him go into heaven"** (Acts 1:1-11).

"According to the working of his great might that he worked in Christ when **he raised him from the dead and seated him at his right hand in the heavenly places**, far above all rule and authority and power and dominion, and above every name that is named, not only in this age but also in the one to come. And he put all things under his feet and gave him as head over all things to the church" (Ephesians 1:19-22).

CHAPTER 4 Questions for Thought and Discussion

1. What implications are there that so many Old Testament Scriptures prophesy about Jesus' life on earth thousands of years before He was born?

2. How does the life of Jesus prove that He was man and that He is God?

3. Why do you think the spiritual leaders of the day wanted Jesus crucified?

4. What is the evidence that Jesus died and rose from the dead?

   Is it enough evidence to convince you that He did die and rise again

5. What does this evidence tell us about Jesus?

   Is it enough evidence that He must be the Son of God? Why or why not?

6. If Jesus did indeed die and rise from the dead, what response does that elicit from you?

CHAPTER 5

The Mystery of Christ Jesus

"Now to him who is able to strengthen you according to my gospel and the preaching of **Jesus Christ**, according to the revelation of the **mystery** that was kept secret for long ages but has now been disclosed" (Romans 16:25-26).

"When you read this, you can perceive my insight into **the mystery of Christ**." (Ephesians 3:4).

"**This mystery** is profound, and I am saying that it **refers to Christ** and the church" (Ephesians 5:32).

"The **mystery** hidden for ages and generations but now revealed to his saints. To them God chose to make known... the riches of the glory of **this mystery, which is Christ** in you, the hope of glory" (Colossians 1:26-27).

"**God's mystery, which is Christ**, in whom are hidden all the treasures of wisdom and knowledge" (Colossians 2:2-3).

"That God may open to us a door for the word, to declare **the mystery of Christ**" (Colossians 4:3).

More than seven times in the New Testament, Jesus is referred to as "the mystery!" All the mysteries from the foundation of the world have to do with Jesus Christ because, according to the Godhead, Jesus is central—He has supremacy or first place in everything (see Colossians 1:18). Consequently, the entire Scripture is pointing to and talking about Christ Jesus. This was not completely clear to the Old Testament readers, but when the New Testament was written, it began to reveal that all the prophecies of the Old Testament were mysteries that had to do with Jesus. Jesus Himself is the fulfillment of almost all of the prophecies of the Old Testament and the mysteries the people of Israel had been wondering about and waiting for to be disclosed. The Apostle Peter's first sermon after Jesus ascended into heaven was to explain to the Jewish people that Jesus really was God and the Messiah/Christ they had been waiting for: "Let all the house of Israel therefore know for certain that God has made him both Lord and Christ, this Jesus whom you crucified" (Acts 2:36).

Jesus was a mystery to the Old Testament children of Israel, as He hadn't come to earth yet. Later, during Jesus' life on earth, the Jewish people did not realize that He was who God had been talking about. He didn't look like what they were expecting based on the prophecies about Him, nor did He comply with the traditions of men that had taken over. Today we have the Old Testament promises explained for us, and we have the New Testament testimony of Jesus' life and teaching. More than that, we have the Holy Spirit whose job is to teach us all things about Jesus (see John 16:12-14). Today, we can know the mystery of Christ and not miss Him in our own life!

However, it would be easy to miss Jesus again. The mystery of His life, death, and resurrection is that it doesn't look like the way man would do things. In Jesus, God confounds the wisdom of the world and reveals the mysterious wisdom of God! God's ways are not our ways, nor are His thoughts our thoughts (see Isaiah 55:8-9); therefore, the way of salvation in Jesus is not what we expect—it is backwards from the system of this world. Rather than Jesus defeating the Romans and reigning triumphantly as an earthly king for Israel, He suffered, was beaten, crucified, and buried. God chose what looks foolish, weak, lowly, and despised in the worldly system. Likewise, God's way of salvation for us today is to put our trust in God rather than ourselves and follow God's ways rather than man's. When we follow Jesus' way rather than the world's way, we look foolish and weak, and are despised by the world. God's wisdom in His way of salvation is not the world's wisdom, but it is a mystery that is of God and can only be discerned by pursuing Him.

> "Yet among the mature we do impart wisdom, although it is not a wisdom of this age or of the rulers of this age, who are doomed to pass away. But **we impart a secret and hidden wisdom of God,** which God decreed before the ages for our glory. None of the rulers of this age understood this, for if they had, they would not have crucified the Lord of glory" (1 Corinthians 1:6-8).

> "But **God chose what is foolish in the world to shame the wise; God chose what is weak in the world to shame the strong; God chose**

what is low and despised in the world, even things that are not, to bring to nothing things that are, so that no human being might boast in the presence of God. And because of him you are in Christ Jesus, who became to us wisdom from God, righteousness and sanctification and redemption, so that, as it is written, "Let the one who boasts, boast in the Lord" (1 Corinthians 2:27-31).

So, what is the mystery of Jesus Christ? The mystery of Christ is that almighty, all-knowing, all-powerful Creator of the universe, solar systems, ecosystems, the complexities of the human body, all the way down to the marvel of a living cell; this Creator God, humbled Himself and became man with all man's limitations in order to take the place of all of humanity. He lived a perfect life in our place, and took the punishment for all of our sin by dying on the cross.

"Christ Jesus, who, though he was in the form of God, **did not count equality with God a thing to be grasped**, but **made himself nothing**, taking the form of a servant, being born in the likeness of men. And **being found in human form, he humbled himself** by becoming obedient to the point of death, even death on a cross." (Philippians 2:5-8).

"**Therefore, he had to be made like his brothers in every respect,** so that he might become a merciful and faithful high priest in the service of God, to make propitiation *[take the wrath of God]* for the sins of the people" (Hebrews 2:17).

The mystery of Christ is that a holy and righteous God, who knew no sin, became sin for us, bearing all of our sin in His sinless body! Not only all of our sin but also all the guilt, shame and pain of our sin that even makes us cringe and want to escape it. More than that, the loving God, who lived in perfect unity with the Father since before the beginning of the world, endured the wrath of God which had been directed at our sin, and suffered the complete separation from God which sin causes...in our place. So that when He rose from the dead, He could impart His righteousness and abundant life to us and restore our relationship to the Father.

"For our sake he made **him to be sin who knew no sin**, so that in him we might become the righteousness of God" (2 Corinthians 5:17).

"**He himself bore our sins in his body** on the tree, that we might die to sin and live to righteousness" (1 Peter 2:24).

"Since, therefore, we have now been justified by his blood, much more shall we be **saved by him from the wrath of God**" (Romans 5:9).

What would make Him do it? The only answer is love! The greatest part of the mystery, worthy of all awe and wonder, is Jesus's unconditional limitless love for us...love that would cause Him to humble Himself, suffer and die in our place.

"For **God so loved the world**, that he gave his only Son, that whoever believes in him should not perish but have eternal life" (John 3:16).

"**God shows his love for us** in that while we were still sinners, Christ died for us" (Romans 5:8).

"**By this we know love**, that he laid down his life for us" (1John 3:16)

His love truly amazing! Let us look more closely now at what actually was accomplished in this mystery of Jesus laying down His life for us.

The Mystery of Jesus' Death on the Cross:

1.   **Forgiveness of sins**

Why Jesus came to earth to die is answered by another mystery set up before the foundation of the world. It was predetermined that the consequence of sin is death, and that the cost to redeem a life from death is another life. When the agreements were made before the foundation of the world, it was predetermined that blood, essentially the death of a life, could make atonement for another life. The mystery required that blood be shed to pay for sin committed because life is in the blood. Atonement means to cover sin in order to bring us back into relationship with God, and to pacify, appease, pardon the wrath of God and punishment against sin that is due us. This was pictured over and over again in the Old Testament sacrifice of animals which took the punishment of sin in the place of man. In Old Testament times there was an elaborate protocol in the tabernacle and temple established for the people of Israel to bring an animal to sacrifice for forgiveness of their sins.

"**For the life of the flesh is in the blood, and I have given it for you on the altar to make atonement for your souls, for it is the blood that makes atonement by the life**" (Leviticus 17:11).

"Indeed, under the law almost everything is purified with blood, and without the shedding of blood there is no forgiveness of sins" (Hebrews 9:22).

Though blood was required, the Old Testament sacrifice of animals was inadequate to take away sin, it only temporarily set aside sin or caused God to pass over sin (see Romans 3:25) until Jesus would come and completely forgive, remove, take away sin for all time. Consequently, the sacrifices had to be made again and again, day after day, year after year. In the Old Testament, God had meant the sacrificial system to be a picture to help His people understand the need for blood to pay for their sin. It was to give them the theology to understand what Jesus would one day come to do for them by dying on the cross. It was to help them see their need for a Savior and look forward to the Messiah. So, the entire sacrifice system of the Old Testament was to illustrate the mystery that Christ Jesus would come to sacrifice His own perfect life, shedding His blood in order to completely remove and deliver us from our sin.

"And every priest stands daily at his service, offering repeatedly the same sacrifices, which can never take away sins. But when Christ had offered for all time a single sacrifice for sins, he sat down at the right hand of God...then he adds, **"I will remember their sins and their lawless deeds no more." Where there is forgiveness of these, there is no longer any offering for sin**" (Hebrews 10:11-12, 18-19).

2. **Justification**

"And you, who were dead in your trespasses and the uncircumcision of your flesh, God made us alive together with him, **having forgiven us all our trespasses, by canceling the record of debt that stood against us with its legal demands. This he set aside, nailing it to the cross**" (Colossians 2:13-14).

In the forgiveness of our sins is included our "justification" which means the canceling of our debt and thereby our acquittal, declaring us not guilty. In so doing all judgment, punishment, and condemnation is taken away. God canceled the record of our debt and all the legal demands of the law, by nailing it to the cross. Because Jesus took our debt upon Himself and fulfilled the requirements of the law, we can escape the judgment and punishment of our sin. "The one who hears My word, and believes Him who sent Me, has eternal life, and does not come into judgment, but has passed out of death into life" (John 5:24). God condemned our sin in Jesus' flesh so that we would no longer stand condemned. Condemnation means to exercise the consequences of law against someone. Condemnation is the justly earned judgment of our sin, yet this verse declares that there is "no condemnation" for those who are in Christ Jesus.

> **"There is therefore now no condemnation for those who are in Christ Jesus**. For the law of the Spirit of life **has set you free in Christ Jesus from the law of sin and death**. For God has done what the law, weakened by the flesh, could not do. By sending his own Son in the likeness of sinful flesh and for sin, he condemned sin in the flesh, in order that **the righteous requirement of the law might be fulfilled in us**, who walk not according to the flesh but according to the Spirit" (Romans 8:1-4).

Besides having our sin completely removed, the requirements of the law met, and judgment of our sin paid for by the blood of Jesus; we also stand in Jesus' righteousness, and are declared righteous instead of guilty! In Christ's death on the cross He restored a right standing for us before God and we are clothed in His white robe of righteousness.

> "For our sake he made him to be sin who knew no sin, so **that in him we might become the righteousness of God**" (2 Corinthians 5:21).

> "I will greatly rejoice in the LORD; my soul shall exult in my God, for he has clothed me with the garments of salvation; **he has covered me with the robe of righteousness**" (Isaiah 61:10).

3. Conquered the power of sin over us

> "We know that our old self was crucified with him **in order that the body of sin might be brought to nothing, so that we would no longer be enslaved to sin**. For one who has died has been **set free from sin . . .** So, you also must consider yourselves dead to sin and alive to God in Christ Jesus. Let not sin therefore reign in your mortal body; to make you obey its passions" (Romans 6:6-7, 11-12).

Thirdly, on the cross, Jesus did not just die to forgive sin and declare us righteous but He conquered sin, death, and the devil so that sin would no longer have power over us. When we embrace the cross and surrender our lives to Christ, it is as if we have died with Christ on the cross and thereby died to sin, free from the power of sin over our life. Jesus frees us from slavery to sin when we submit our life to His and receive His work on the cross. At the same time, Jesus offers us His life in exchange for our life so that we are able to resist sin in the future. That means we don't have to continue in our sin, sinful habits, or addictions. Jesus came to cancel the power of sin over us.

"Therefore, if anyone is in Christ, **he is a new creation. The old has passed away; behold, the new has come**" (2 Corinthians 5:17).

4. **Redeemed us from the consequences of sin**

Not only did Jesus' death forgive the sins we committed and disarm sin's power over us, but on the cross Jesus also bore the consequences of our sins. Jesus knows and experienced in His death on the cross all the pain and suffering our sin has caused us. This means that we do not have to reap all of the consequences that we have sown if we take these sins to Jesus. In Jesus' death, we have been redeemed from the consequences and curse of sin and do not have to suffer what we really deserve. To redeem means to "buy back" and is associated with paying for a slave to give him his freedom. Redemption in Jesus' death is the means of healing the damage sin has caused us and gaining freedom from the consequences of sin.

"**Christ redeemed us from the curse of the law** by becoming a curse for us—for it is written, 'Cursed is everyone who is hanged on a tree'" (Galatians 3:13).

Likewise, Jesus bore the consequence of the sin that other people have committed against us, and there is also healing for the pain and suffering other people's sin has caused us. When Jesus died on the cross, He suffered the experience of all our sins in His body as well as the sins that were committed against us. He knows all of our suffering from sin intimately, along with all of the broken relationships, rejection, shame, and guilt sin has caused. He carried all of our suffering in Himself so that when we come to Him, He is able to heal us of our pain.

"**Surely, he has borne our griefs and carried our sorrows**; yet we esteemed him stricken, smitten by God, and afflicted. But he was wounded for our transgressions; he was crushed for our iniquities;

upon him was the chastisement that brought us peace, and with his stripes we are healed" (Isaiah 53:4-5).

5. Reconciled our relationship with God

The biggest problem with our sin is that it has separated us from God. Jesus' death on the cross paid the price for sin that we would no longer be separated from Him. The whole reason God forgave our sins is so He could restore relationship with us again—to reconcile our relationship. Jesus died that He might bring us back to God. God illustrated this while Jesus was dying on the cross by tearing the curtain in the temple in two from top to bottom (see Matthew 27:51). This curtain used to separate the people from the Holy Place where God's presence dwelled. The day Jesus died, God demonstrated that we no longer need to be separated from His presence.

"For Christ also suffered once for sins, the righteous for the unrighteous, **that he might bring us to God**, being put to death in the flesh but made alive in the spirit" (1 Peter 3:18).

"In Christ God was reconciling the world to himself, not counting their trespasses against them…We implore you on behalf of Christ, be reconciled to God. For our sake he made him to be sin who knew no sin, so that in him we might become the righteousness of God" (2 Corinthians 5:19-21).

"For in him all the fullness of God was pleased to dwell, and **through him to reconcile to himself all things, whether on earth or in heaven, making peace by the blood of his cross**. And you, who once were alienated and hostile in mind, doing evil deeds, he has now reconciled in his body of flesh by his death, in order to present you holy and blameless and above reproach before him" (Colossians 1:19-22).

Reconciliation means to restore our relationship so that we could again walk with God like Adam did in the garden. It wasn't enough for Jesus that we would be forgiven and set free from sin. In the moment of our forgiveness, He restores our relationship with Him and calls us His friends. He says that He loves us so much that He does not want us as servants but that He has chosen us to be His friend. How awesome is that!

"Greater love has no one than this that someone lay down his life for his friends. you are my friends if you do what I command you. **No longer do I call you servants**, for the servant does not know what his master is doing; **but I have called you friends**, for all that I have heard from my Father I have made known to you. You did not choose me, but I chose you" (John 15:13-16).

6. **Regenerated us from death to life**

"He saved us, not because of works done by us in righteousness, but according to his own mercy, **by the washing of regeneration and renewal of the Holy Spirit**" (Titus 3:5).

When Jesus died on the cross, He didn't stay there or in the tomb, He rose from the dead three days later and showed Himself to over 500 of His followers. It is because of Jesus' resurrection that we can have new life, which begins the day we surrender our life to Him as our Savior and continues through eternity. It is eternal life with God that we can begin to participate in the minute we invite Jesus into our life. Jesus' resurrection proves He was victorious over sin, death, and the devil. In His resurrection, Jesus overcame death so that we possess Jesus' life in us the moment we invite Him into our life. Not only do we have life with God now on earth, but we will not die, but will have everlasting life.

"For God so loved the world, that He gave His only Son, so that everyone who believes in Him **will not perish, but have eternal life**" (John 3:16).

"Truly, truly, I say to you, whoever hears my word and believes him who sent me **has eternal life**. He does not come into judgment, but has **passed from death to life**" (John 5:24).

"For if while we were enemies we were reconciled to God by the death of his Son, much more, **now that we are reconciled, shall we be saved by his life**" (Romans 5:9-10).

"Just as Christ was raised from the dead by the glory of the Father, **we too might walk in newness of life**. For if we have been united with him in a death like his, we shall certainly be **united with him in a resurrection like his**. Now if we have died with Christ, we believe that **we will also live with him**" (Romans 6:4-5, 8).

This life is like the life that Adam had with God before the Fall. This life is the life of Jesus living in us, to empower us to connect with God and receive all that God has for us. "Christ in you, the hope of glory" (Colossians 1:27). To be full of Jesus' Spirit makes us spiritually alive, here on earth and into eternity. We no longer have to depend on the knowledge of good and evil for "we have the mind of Christ" (1 Corinthians 2:16). His Spirit in us enables us to overcome sin in our lives, to manifest the life of Jesus living through us (see 2 Corinthians 4:10-11) and to do the good works that Jesus did while He was on the earth (see John 14:12). His Spirit in us fills us and keeps us connected to God, abundantly full of resurrection life while we walk this earth.

"I came that they may have life and have it abundantly" (John 10:10).

The life of Jesus in us is eternal so that we will live forever with Him. In contrast to the last chapter where we defined "death" as: "suffering the punishment of eternal destruction, away from the presence of the Lord and from the glory of his might" (see 2 Thessalonians 1:7-9); "life" is eternity in the presence of the Lord in all of His glory! Our physical death will really be the beginning of living when "what is mortal will be swallowed up by life" (2 Corinthians 5:4).

7. Defeated the Devil

"I will put enmity between you [*Satan*] and the woman, and between your offspring and her offspring [*Jesus*]; he [*Jesus*] shall bruise your [*Satan*] head, and you shall bruise his [*Jesus'*] heel" (Genesis 3:15).

From the foundation of the world, the mystery of Christ was hidden. However, as early as the Fall when Adam and Eve ate the fruit, God brought glimpses of revelation to the mystery of Christ, although it was still hidden in metaphor. At the Fall, God spoke the above verse to Satan who was disguising himself as a snake. God prophesied that Jesus' heel would crush Satan's head. This meant that Jesus' death and resurrection would ultimately defeat Satan, take back Satan's dominion over the world, and strip him of all power and authority. From the beginning of creation, God had a plan to rescue us when we sinned. From the beginning, God planned to justly fulfill the blood requirement with the blood of His own Son Jesus. Jesus' blood would nullify the consequences of our sin and take back the dominion Satan had taken over us and the whole world. Through Jesus' death, the Bible says that He destroyed the devil and all of his works, disarming all of the devil's demons and triumphing over them in His death and resurrection.

"Since therefore the children share in flesh and blood, he himself likewise partook of the same things, that **through death he might destroy the one who has the power of death**, that is, the devil, and deliver all those who through fear of death were subject to lifelong slavery" (Hebrews 2:14-15).

"**He disarmed the rulers and authorities and put them to open shame, by triumphing over them in him**" (Colossians 2:15).

"The reason the Son of God appeared was **to destroy the works of the devil**" (1 John 3:8).

In Jesus' death on the cross, He delivered us from lifelong slavery to the devil, rescued us from the kingdom of Satan, and transferred us into 'the Kingdom of God.' When we receive Jesus as Savior, we no longer live under the oppression and authority of the devil. Jesus came to set us free from Satan's captivity. Jesus came to set the captives free and liberate the oppressed.

"The Spirit of the Lord is upon me, because he has anointed me to proclaim good news to the poor. He has sent me to proclaim **liberty to the captives** and recovering of sight to the blind, to set at **liberty those who are oppressed**, to proclaim the year of the Lord's favor" (Luke 4:18-19).

"To open their eyes, so that they may turn from darkness to light and **from the power of Satan to God**, that they may receive forgiveness of sins and a place among those who are sanctified by faith in me" (Acts 26:18).

"He has delivered us **from the domain of darkness and transferred us to the kingdom of his beloved Son**" (Colossians 1:13).

Not only has Jesus rescued and delivered us from the power of Satan, but God has seated Jesus on His throne at His right hand to reign in heavenly places forever. Jesus now rules and has authority over the whole world, over every ruler, authority, power, and dominion including Satan's, whether we acknowledge that fact or not. Jesus' supremacy is the mystery of Christ Jesus that can only be seen with spiritual eyes and the wisdom of God. Jesus reigns!!

"That he worked in Christ when he raised him from the dead and **seated him at his right hand in the heavenly places, far above all rule and authority and power and dominion, and above every name that is named**, not only in this age but also in the one to come" (Ephesians 1:20-21).

"Jesus Christ, who has gone into heaven and is **at the right hand of God, with angels, authorities, and powers having been subjected to him**" (1 Peter 3:22).

CHAPTER 5 Questions for Thought and Discussion

1. Why do you think Jesus is called a "Mystery"?

2. Which of the seven mysteries of Jesus' death on the cross meets the needs of your heart and why?

3. If 'guilt' is a feeling that we have done something wrong, how does Jesus' death on the cross, address guilt? Which verses in the chapter address guilt?

4. If 'shame' is a feeling that something is wrong with us, how does Jesus' death on the cross, address shame? Which verses in the chapter address shame?

5. What does it mean to you to have Jesus reconcile or restore your relationship with God?

6. What does it mean to "not perish but have everlasting life" (John 3:16)?

CHAPTER 6

The Name above All Names

"That He *[God]*worked in Christ when he raised him from the dead and seated him at his right hand in the heavenly places, far above all rule and authority and power and dominion, and **above every name that is named**, not only in this age but also in the one to come" (Ephesians 1:20-21).

"Therefore, God has highly exalted him and bestowed on him **the name that is above every name,** so that at the name of Jesus every knee should bow, in heaven and on earth and under the earth, and every tongue confess that Jesus Christ is Lord, to the glory of God the Father" (Philippians 2:9-11).

Jesus is the "name that is above every name!" Because Jesus humbled Himself and died on the cross, God exalted Him and every knee will bow, and every tongue will confess that Jesus Christ is Lord. Jesus' name is above all other names in this age, in the age to come, in heaven, on earth, and under the earth! His name stands alone above all power and authority and rule and dominion! His name towers over the names of every pagan god, all other religions' gods, and Satan himself. I think that covers everything!

    His is the name every tongue will confess, either before they see Him face to face or when they see Him at His second coming. For those who call on His name before they see Him face to face, they will be saved. For those who will confess His name after they die, it will be too late and result in their eternal damnation for "it is appointed for man to die once, and after that comes judgment" (Hebrews 9:27). Jesus' name is the only name by which we will be saved. There is no other name. There is no other way to God except through Jesus. To be saved, we must call upon the name of Jesus Christ in this life.

"For everyone who calls on the name of the Lord will be saved" (Romans 10:13).

"Jesus said, 'I am the way, and the truth, and the life. No one comes to the Father except through me'" (John 14:6).

"For there is no other name under heaven given among men by which we must be saved" (Acts 4:12).

"For there is one God, and there is one mediator between God and men, the man Christ Jesus, who gave himself as a ransom for all" (1 Timothy 2:5-6).

In Scripture, a name means, "who a person is." Their name describes their nature and character. Names of God reflect how God has chosen to reveal Himself to us in creation, in the Bible, and by sending Jesus to the earth. The names by which God has named Himself and Jesus are not just titles; they are descriptions of how God has acted in relationship with people throughout the history in the Bible and with us now. Most of the names of God in Scripture are in the context of somebody naming God for what He had just done in their lives. To call on the name of Jesus requires us to know who He is and understand what He is doing right now. The depth to which we understand who Jesus is, is the depth that we can call on His name and put our trust in Him. In this chapter, we will focus on who Jesus is so that you know who you are calling on when you call on His name, and so that you have deeper understanding and can trust Him more.

There are many names given to Jesus that describe something about Him, which would be an awesome study. However, there is one predominant title made of three names, which is stated over 80 times in the New Testament and many more times than that separately: Jesus Christ the Lord. Each of these three names: Jesus, Christ, and Lord have specific meanings that describe different aspects of who Jesus is, different aspects that we can come to understand and put our faith in. We are going to study these three so that we can know who we are calling on when we call on the name of Jesus Christ the Lord.

The name "Jesus" means "Jehovah is salvation" or it means "Savior" and "salvation." The name "Christ" in Greek is the same as "Messiah" in Hebrew and it literally means "the anointed one." In the Jewish context, it means the descendent of King David, anointed as King of Israel who will reign forever on the earth. The name "Lord" was the name used of God since creation and means "the One having power and authority." Each of these names: Jesus, Christ, and Lord, are associated with Old Testament prophecies about a man coming from God who would be the way of salvation for the people, the Messiah who is anointed King forever, and is the Lord who reigns with all power and authority! The Jewish people knew exactly who they were waiting for based on Old Testament prophecy which defined these names.

At the announcement of Jesus' birth to Joseph, Mary, and the shepherds, all three of these names were used, so they would have known exactly who the angels were talking about. When the angel announced Jesus' birth to Joseph, His earthly father, the angel told Joseph to name the baby Jesus because He would save His people from their sins. Jesus means "Savior."

> "Joseph, son of David, do not fear to take Mary as your wife, for that which is conceived in her is from the Holy Spirit. She will bear a son, and you shall call his name **Jesus**, for **he will save his people from their sins**" (Matthew 1:20-21).

When the angel announced to Mary that she would be mother to Jesus, he told her three things about the baby she would conceive. His name would be Jesus/Savior, He would be the Son of the Most High which would make Him Lord, and that He would reign on the throne of David forever which would make Him the Christ, the anointed one.

> "Do not be afraid, Mary, for you have found favor with God. And behold, you will conceive in your womb and bear a son, and you shall call his name **Jesus**. He will be great and will be called the **Son of the Most High**. And the **Lord God will give to him the throne of his father David, and he will reign over the house of Jacob forever, and of his kingdom there will be no end**" (Luke 1:30-33).

When the angels announced to the shepherds that a baby had been born, they told the shepherds these same three important things, that the baby was the Savior, that He is the Christ, and that He is Lord.

> "Fear not, for behold, I bring you good news of great joy that will be for all the people. For unto you is born this day in the city of David a **Savior**, who is **Christ** the **Lord**. And this will be a sign for you: you will

find a baby wrapped in swaddling clothes and lying in a manger" (Luke 2:10-12).

At the end of His earthly life, people were still confirming that Jesus was the Savior, Christ, and Lord. When Jesus rode into Jerusalem to celebrate the Passover five days before His death, the multitudes of people in Jerusalem greeted Him by spreading palm branches out on the road before Him, proclaiming Jesus as Savior because Hosanna means "save us," declaring Him to be the Christ because He is the son of David to sit on David's throne, and naming Him as the Lord.

> "And the crowds that went before him and that followed him were shouting, '**Hosanna** to the **Son of David**! Blessed is he who comes in the name of the **Lord! Hosanna** in the highest!'" (Matthew 21:9).

The whole decision as to whether Jesus deserved to be crucified was based on whether or not He claimed to be the Christ, the Son of God. "And the high priest said to him, 'I adjure you by the living God, tell us if you are the Christ, the Son of God'" (Matthew 26:63). Because the High Priest did not believe Jesus was Lord and Christ, it made sense to him to crucify Jesus for claiming to be the Christ, the Son of God.

> "Again, the high priest asked him, 'Are you the Christ, the Son of the Blessed?' And Jesus said, 'I am, and you will see the Son of Man seated at the right hand of Power, and coming with the clouds of heaven.' And the high priest tore his garments and said, 'What further witnesses do we need? You have heard his blasphemy. What is your decision?' And they all condemned him as deserving death" (Mark 14:61-64).

By the time Jesus died on the cross, the issue had become that Jesus could not just be a good teacher or a prophet because He Himself declared that He was the Christ, the Son of God, and Lord, and quoted a prophecy found in Daniel 7:13-14 regarding the Christ who would rule with all power and authority forever. If He was not the Christ, the Lord God, He would be a liar and deceiver deserving of death because He claimed to be God. Jesus's many declarations that He is the Savior, the Christ, the Lord completely eliminates Him from just being a good man, teacher, or prophet, as some people still want to believe about Him. Either He is an evil liar that should not deserve our respect or He is who He says He is, Jesus Christ the Lord, which makes Him God.

It was the greatest irony that at Jesus' death, Pilate nailed a sign on the cross over His head stating what is actually true: "This is Jesus, the King of the Jews" (see Matthew 27:37). However, the whole reason the Jews at that time wanted to crucify Jesus was because they didn't believe He was their Savior or King but rather He was a blasphemer by saying He was the Christ. God prevailed and had the last word that this man whom they crucified was actually the Savior and Christ, King of the Jews.

Later, after Jesus had ascended into heaven, the disciples waited in Jerusalem until the day called Pentecost, which was a Jewish holiday that brought Jews from all around the world to Jerusalem. In the power of the Holy Spirit, the Apostle Peter addressed the crowds and explained to all the visiting Jews what had just happened in Jerusalem. He told them that a man named Jesus had come, been crucified, raised from the dead, and ascended into heaven to sit at the right hand of God as Lord, which Peter argued proved Jesus was the Christ who would live forever. Peter attested that Jesus was the Savior, Christ, and Lord that they had been waiting for and challenged the people to give their life to Jesus as their Savior, Christ, and Lord.

> "Let all the house of Israel therefore know for certain that God has made him both **Lord** and **Christ**, this **Jesus** whom you crucified" (Acts 2:36).

Savior

We translate the name "Jesus" from "Yeshua" which means "salvation" and includes many aspects of salvation: help, rescue, deliverance, health, refuge, welfare, healing. So, the words "save" or "savior" encompasses many aspects of meeting all kinds of our needs, physical and spiritual. In the last chapter, we began to describe the saving work of Jesus in dying on the cross. We saw Jesus as the Savior who by His death on the cross took our punishment and forgives our sins which include defeating the power of sin in our lives, removing the consequence of sin that we committed and the sins of those who have sinned against us, reconciling our relationship with God, giving us new life in the sense of abundant life on this earth as well as eternal life after death, and finally disarming the power of the devil over our lives and transferring us into the Kingdom of God. Included in that is emotional and physical healing for the wounds sin has caused, rescue and deliverance from the problems that sin has produced in our lives, as well as good news like protection and provision for all of our needs. There is so much included in the saving work of the cross we will literally spend eternity growing in our understanding of all that is encompassed in the work of Jesus on the cross to save us. Not only that, but in His resurrection from the dead, He conquered death and the devil who held the keys to death, and provides us abundant life on earth and eternal life with Jesus.

In the beginning of Jesus' ministry, in His first appearance found in Luke 4, we find Jesus introducing Himself as Savior. There were many other prophecies that Jesus fulfills, but rather than choosing a prophecy about the Messiah reigning as King on David's throne forever, or other prophecies about Himself as God with all power and authority, Jesus introduced Himself as Savior. Jesus read out loud the passage from Isaiah 61:1-2 and declared that He is the fulfillment of this passage.

> "And he came to Nazareth, where he had been brought up. And as was his custom, he went to the synagogue on the Sabbath day, and he stood up to read. And the scroll of the prophet Isaiah was given to him. He unrolled the scroll and found the place where it was written, 'The Spirit of the Lord is upon me, because he has anointed me **to proclaim good news to the poor.** He has sent me **to proclaim liberty to the captives** and **recovering of sight to the blind, to set at liberty those who are oppressed, to proclaim the year of the Lord's favor**.' And he rolled up the scroll and gave it back to the attendant and sat down. And the eyes of all in the synagogue were fixed on him. And he began to say to them, 'Today this Scripture has been fulfilled in your hearing'" (Luke 4:16-21).

Instead of focusing on His victorious reign as King on David's throne, which the Israelites were waiting for and looking forward to, or His rightful position as the Lord, the Son of God, Jesus focused on His heart for the poor, the captive, the blind, and the oppressed. Jesus didn't come for people who had it all together and were successful, for the healthy and those who had no need for a Savior. He came for the needy, for the oppressed, for the lost, for the sick. He came to save sinners.

> "**For the Son of Man has come to save that which was lost**" (Matthew 18:11).

> "And when Jesus heard it, he said to them, 'Those who are well have no need of a physician, but those who are sick. **I came not to call the righteous, but sinners**'" (Mark 2:17).

> "**Christ Jesus came into the world to save sinners**" (1 Timothy 1:15).

What He promises is to bring good news, liberty, recovery, and God's favor to people who are spiritually poor, blind, captive and oppressed. He offers salvation in every form that a spiritually desperate person would need. This requires admitting our need for a Savior. It requires admitting that we are poor, blind, captive, and oppressed; that we need deliverance, to be rescued; that we need good news and God's favor. In the following verses, Jesus is offering spiritual wealth, covering, and sight to those who admit they need it.

> "For you say, I am rich, I have prospered, and I need nothing, not realizing that you are wretched, pitiable, poor, blind, and naked. I counsel you to buy from me gold refined by fire, so that you may be rich, and white garments so that you may clothe yourself and the shame of your nakedness may not be seen, and salve to anoint your eyes, so that you may see" (Revelation 3:17-18).

Let us recognize our need for a Savior like the tax collector in this story that Jesus told. In the following story, the tax collector realized his absolute helplessness and complete neediness before God, and all he could say was, "be merciful to me a sinner"; 'have pity on me for I am in need of You.' The tax collector admitted his sin and cried out for mercy, and he was saved. For Jesus "is able to save to the uttermost those who draw near to God through him" (Hebrews 7:25). The tax collector is contrasted to the Pharisee who is proud, independent, and self-righteous, dependent on his own good works, apparently not aware of his need of God or anything God could do for him.

> "He also told this parable to some who trusted in themselves that they were righteous, and treated others with contempt: 'Two men went up into the temple to pray, one a Pharisee and the other a tax collector. The Pharisee, standing by himself, prayed thus: 'God, I thank you that I am not like other men, extortioners, unjust, adulterers, or even like this tax collector. I fast twice a week; I give tithes of all that I get.' But the tax collector, standing far off, would not even lift up his eyes to heaven, but beat his breast, saying, 'God, be merciful to me, a sinner!' I tell you; this man went down to his house justified, rather than the other'" (Luke 18:9-13).

Lord

> "*He is the image of the invisible God, the firstborn of all creation*. For **by him all things were created, in heaven and on earth, visible and**

invisible, whether thrones or dominions or rulers or authorities—all things were created through him and for him. And he is <u>before all things, and in him all things hold together</u>…, that in everything he might be preeminent. For in him all the fullness of God was pleased to dwell" **(Colossians 1:15-19).**

"Long ago, at many times and in many ways, God spoke to our fathers by the prophets, but in these last days he has spoken to us by his Son, whom he appointed the heir of all things, **through whom also he created the world.** *He is the radiance of the glory of God and the exact imprint of his nature*, and <u>he upholds the universe by the word of his power</u>" (Hebrews 1:1-3).

Both of these verses tell us three things about Jesus being Lord, which means that He is the One with all the power and authority: He created all things, sustains all things, and He is the exact image of God.

First, Jesus created all things. Jesus is God and has been with God the Father and Holy Spirit since before the foundation of the earth. In the beginning of the world, Jesus, as part of the Godhead, created all things in the heaven and earth. He was in the beginning with God. "All things were made through him, and without him was not anything made that was made" (John 1:2-3). And the above two verses are clear that Jesus is the creator of all things. As creator of all things in the universe, we see the power and glory and authority Jesus has. As our Lord, Jesus has that same power and authority to work and move on our behalf. The power and authority Jesus had to create the entire universe is the same power and authority He has today over everything in our world and lives.

Secondly, Jesus did not just create the world to set it into motion and function independently of Himself, rather the whole universe is dependent on Jesus right now. These two verses say that in Jesus "all things hold together" and "he upholds the universe by the word of his power." Jesus is the strong force that holds every atom together! Jesus is the one who keeps the ecosystems in balance and maintains them! Jesus is the power holding the solar system in its place. Jesus is intimately involved with each person's life and circumstance. Even in the end times when everything looks to be out of balance, the solar system shifts its place, or our circumstances spiral out of our control, Jesus will be completely in control! In fact, He even told us ahead of time in Scripture what He is going to be doing in the end times. (See the last book of the Bible, the Revelation of Jesus.) He upholds all things by the word of His power!

Third, Jesus is the exact "image" or representation of God the Father; "the exact imprint of His nature; the radiance of His glory." God the Father is invisible so Jesus is how God the Father has spoken to us, to reveal Himself to us. The fullness of God the Father dwells in Jesus. Jesus is God. Jesus explained to His disciples that since they had seen and knew Jesus, they had also seen and knew God the Father because He was in the Father and the Father was in Him. Jesus claimed that it was God the Father that dwelled in Him that enabled Him to do the works that He did.

> "Jesus said to him, 'I am the way, and the truth, and the life. No one comes to the Father except through me. If you had known me, you would have known my Father also. From now on you do know him and have seen him.' Philip said to him, 'Lord, show us the Father, and it is enough for us.' Jesus said to him, 'Have I been with you so long, and you still do not know me, Philip? **Whoever has seen me has seen the Father**. How can you say, 'Show us the Father'? **Do you not believe that I am in the Father and the Father is in me? The words that I say to you I do not speak on my own authority, but the Father who dwells in me does his works. Believe me that I am in the Father and the Father is in me, or else believe on account of the works themselves'"** (John 14:6-11).

Jesus' Signs Prove that He is God

The works that the Father did through His Son, Jesus, proved that Jesus was one with the Father and that He has all power and authority as Lord. Jesus challenged His followers many times to believe that He was God based on the miraculous signs and wonders that He did.

> "But the testimony that I have is greater than that of John. For the **works** that the Father has given me to accomplish, the very **works** that I am doing, **bear witness about me that the Father has sent me**" (John 5:36).

> "If I am not doing the works of my Father, then do not believe me; but if I do them, even though you do not believe me, **believe the works**, that you may know and understand that the Father is in me and I am in the Father" (John 10:37-38).

"Believe me that I am in the Father and the Father is in me, or else **believe on account of the works themselves**" (John 14:11).

"Men of Israel, hear these words: Jesus of Nazareth, **a man attested to you by God with mighty works and wonders and signs that God did through him** in your midst, as you yourselves know" (Acts 2:22).

Jesus is indeed God come in human flesh to prove He has the power and authority to save us from our sin. Once while on earth, Jesus received a lot of opposition for offering to forgive a man's sins. As Savior and Lord, Jesus has power to forgive sins. So that doubters would know that the Son of Man has authority on earth to forgive sins, Jesus also healed the man of paralysis. Jesus who has power and authority over disease also has power and authority to save us from our sins.

"And behold, some people brought to him a paralytic, lying on a bed. And when Jesus saw their faith, he said to the paralytic, 'Take heart, my son; your sins are forgiven.' And behold, some of the scribes said to themselves, 'This man is blaspheming.' But Jesus, knowing their thoughts, said, 'Why do you think evil in your hearts? For which is easier, to say, 'Your sins are forgiven,' or to say, 'Rise and walk'? **But that you may know that the Son of Man has authority on earth to forgive sins**"—he then said to the paralytic— **'Rise, pick up your bed and go home.' And he rose and went home.** When the crowds saw it, they were afraid, and they glorified God, who had given such authority to men" (Matthew 9:2-8).

In the gospels, there are 37 different miracles fully recorded, besides the fact that many times throughout Jesus' three years of ministry it says that Jesus went about healing every disease and casting out demons.

"And he went throughout all Galilee, teaching in their synagogues and proclaiming the gospel of the kingdom and **healing every disease and every affliction** among the people. So his fame spread throughout all Syria, and they brought him all the sick, those afflicted with various diseases and pains, those oppressed by demons, epileptics, and paralytics, and **he healed them**" (Matthew 4:23-24).

"And Jesus went throughout all the cities and villages, teaching in their synagogues and proclaiming the gospel of the kingdom and **healing every disease and every affliction**" (Matthew 9:35).

Jesus has been doing miracles and healings since the beginning of His ministry on earth. In the name of Jesus, miracles still happen today and still prove that Jesus is Lord and has all power and authority. Because Jesus not only created the world but also sustains and empowers it by the word of His mouth, we can expect our prayers to be answered and miracles to happen today in Jesus' name: in His power and authority. Jesus promises that in His name we can ask anything and it will be done. Since we have no power or authority in and of ourselves, when we call on His name as Lord, we are calling on His power and authority as God. We can expect His power to be as great as His power was when He created the whole world! It is His same creative, sustaining power as the Lord, that works in our world today.

> "**Whatever you ask in my name, this I will do**, that the Father may be glorified in the Son. **If you ask me anything in my name, I will do it**" (John 14:13-14).

> "**Whatever you ask the Father in my name, he may give it to you**" (John 15:16).

> "Truly, truly, I say to you, **whatever you ask of the Father in my name, he will give it to you.** Until now you have asked nothing in my name. Ask, and you will receive, that your joy may be full" (John 16:23-24).

While Jesus was on earth, He sent His disciples out to tell the good news about Jesus and also to heal the sick and cast out demons in His name (see Matthew 10:1, Luke 9:1). After Jesus ascended into heaven, He told His disciples to wait in Jerusalem for the power of the Holy Spirit to come upon them (see Acts 1:8). Since then, Jesus has continued to do miracles and signs when His followers call on His name to attest to the truth of the testimony about who Jesus is to this day. Today God is continuing to answer prayers, heal the sick, cast out demons, and do signs and wonders in His name to confirm that Jesus is indeed God. According to these verses, there is a purpose why Jesus does the signs and wonders and that is to confirm the message that Jesus is Savior, Christ, and Lord so that we don't miss this great salvation!

> "And they went out and preached everywhere, while the Lord worked with them and **confirmed the message by accompanying signs**" (Mark 16:20).

> "How shall we escape if we neglect such a great salvation? It was declared at first by the Lord, and it was attested to us by those who

heard, while **God also bore witness by signs and wonders and various miracles** and by gifts of the Holy Spirit distributed according to his will" (Hebrews 2:3-4).

Jesus Reigning as Lord God

According to the following verses, Jesus is now seated at the right hand of God in heaven, having all power and authority as the Lord God. From His place in heaven, at the right hand of God, He exerts His power and authority over the whole earth and is waiting His return to earth.

"According to the working of his great might that he worked in Christ when he raised him from the dead and **seated him at his right hand in the heavenly places**, far above all rule and authority and power and dominion, and above every name that is named, not only in this age but also in the one to come" (Ephesians 1:19-21).

"After making purification for sins, **he sat down at the right hand of the Majesty on high**, having become as much superior to angels as the name he has inherited is more excellent than theirs" (Hebrews 1:3).

"Now the point in what we are saying is this: we have such a high priest, one who is **seated at the right hand of the throne of the Majesty in heaven**" (Hebrews 8:1).

"But when Christ had offered for all time a single sacrifice for sins, **he sat down at the right hand of God**" (Hebrews 10:12).

When John, the author of the Book of Revelation, saw Jesus, he described Him with His head and hair as white as wool, His eyes like flames of fire, His feet like burnished bronze, and His voice the sound of many waters. In His right hand, He had seven stars, out of His mouth came a two-edged sword, and His face was shining like the sun. This is a picture of the glorified Jesus where He currently is, sitting in heaven to the right hand of God the Father, reigning as Lord over heaven and earth.

"Then I turned to see the voice that was speaking to me, and on turning I saw seven golden lampstands, and in the midst of the lampstands one like a son of man, clothed with a long robe and with a golden sash around his chest. The hairs of his head were white, like white wool, like snow. His eyes were like a flame of fire, his feet were like burnished bronze, refined in a furnace, and his voice was like the roar of many waters. In his right hand he held seven stars, from his mouth came a sharp two-edged sword, and his face was like the sun shining in full strength. When I saw him, I fell at his feet as though dead. But he laid his right hand on me, saying, "Fear not, I am the first and the last, and the living one. I died, and behold I am alive forevermore, and I have the keys of Death and Hades" (Revelation 1:13-18).

When John saw this revelation of Jesus, he fell at His feet as though dead! If you were to see Jesus now, what would you do? Would you fall face down at His feet? Would you bow your knee at the sound of His name? Will you call out the name of Jesus and confess that Jesus Christ is both Savior and Lord?

Christ

The Lord Jesus is reigning over heaven and earth as He awaits His return to earth as Christ, the Messiah, to fill the throne of David and reign forever and ever. This is the fulfillment of many prophecies like 1 Samuel 2:35, 1 Samuel 7:13-16, and Psalm 89:3,4 which promise that God will raise up an Anointed One of the line of King David whose kingdom will never end but will be established forever. That is why the New Testament opens with the lineage of Jesus; it is so important to prove that Jesus is of the house and lineage of David!

Let's look more closely at one prophecy in Isaiah about the coming Christ the Messiah. Around 800 years before Christ was born, Isaiah prophesied that Jesus would be born and the government would be on His shoulder, and that His government would continue to increase and never end. He would sit on the throne of King David and reign in peace, with justice and righteousness forever. This prophecy speaks of Jesus' first coming as a baby in Bethlehem and also speaks of Jesus' second coming as triumphant King who will rule the earth forever into eternity with justice and righteousness.

"For to us a child is born, to us a son is given;
and the government shall be upon his shoulder,
and his name shall be called Wonderful Counselor,
Mighty God, Everlasting Father, Prince of Peace.

Of the increase of his government and of peace there will be no end,
on the throne of David and over his kingdom,
to establish it and to uphold it with justice and with righteousness
from this time forth and forevermore.
The zeal of the LORD of hosts will do this" (Isaiah 9:6-7).

The Old Testament prophesies Jesus' second coming many times. The prophet Daniel prophesied that Jesus would come with the clouds of heaven as the Son of Man, a name which Jesus used many times in the Gospels referring to when He comes back at the second coming. Daniel prophesied that Jesus would be given all dominion and glory on earth which would birth an everlasting Kingdom that would never end.

"I saw in the night visions, and behold, with the clouds of heaven
there came one like a **son of man**, and he came to the Ancient of Days
and was presented before him.
And to him was given dominion and glory and a kingdom,
that all peoples, nations, and languages should serve him;
his dominion is an everlasting dominion, which shall not pass away,
and his kingdom one that shall not be destroyed" (Daniel 7:13-14).

This is the prophecy from Daniel that Jesus quoted when He was being interrogated by the High Priest before His crucifixion. Jesus quoted this passage referring to Himself as the "Son of Man" claiming to be the Christ who would be seated at the right hand of God and then come to earth on the clouds of heaven.

"And the high priest said to him, 'I adjure you by the living God, tell us
if you are the Christ, the Son of God.' Jesus said to him, 'You have said
so. But I tell you, **from now on you will see the Son of Man seated at**
the right hand of Power and coming on the clouds of heaven'"
(Matthew 26:63-64).

In the Gospels, Jesus prophesied that when He returns, we would all see Him coming as the glorified "Son of Man" riding on the clouds as He comes to bring judgment on the earth and reign as King for eternity.

"For the **Son of Man is going to come with his angels in the glory of**
his Father, and then he will repay each person according to what he
has done" (Matthew 16:27).

> "Immediately after the tribulation of those days the sun will be darkened, and the moon will not give its light, and the stars will fall from heaven, and the powers of the heavens will be shaken. **Then will appear in heaven the sign of the Son of Man, and then all the tribes of the earth will mourn, and they will see the Son of Man coming on the clouds of heaven with power and great glory.** And he will send out his angels with a loud trumpet call, and they will gather his elect from the four winds, from one end of heaven to the other" (Matthew 24:29-31).

At the beginning of the Book of the Revelation of Christ, John describes Jesus as coming on the clouds, with every eye seeing Him.

> "Jesus Christ the faithful witness, the firstborn of the dead, and the ruler of kings on earth. To him who loves us and has freed us from our sins by his blood … to him be glory and dominion forever and ever. Amen. Behold, **he is coming with the clouds, and every eye will see him, even those who pierced him, and all tribes of the earth will wail on account of him.** Even so. Amen. "I am the Alpha and the Omega," says the Lord God, "who is and who was and who is to come, the Almighty" (Revelation 1:5-8).

Why will the tribes of the earth mourn and wail on account of Jesus coming? Because as we said earlier, at the name of Jesus, every knee will bow and every tongue will confess Jesus is Lord, but if this happens for the first time at Jesus' return, it will be too late! It will be the time of judgment and those who have not called on the name of Jesus before the coming of Christ will be judged! At the end of the Book of Revelation is the description of Jesus' triumphant return to earth as King of kings and Lord of lords, with all power and authority to judge and bring justice to the earth by finally destroying all evil.

> "Then I saw heaven opened, and behold, a white horse! The one sitting on it is called Faithful and True, and in righteousness he judges and makes war. His eyes are like a flame of fire, and on his head are many diadems, and he has a name written that no one knows but himself. He is clothed in a robe dipped in blood, and the name by which he is called is The Word of God. And the armies of heaven, arrayed in fine linen, white and pure, were following him on white horses. From his mouth comes a sharp sword with which to strike down the nations, and he will rule them with a rod of iron. He will tread the winepress of

the fury of the wrath of God the Almighty. On his robe and on his thigh he has a name written, King of kings and Lord of lords" (Revelation 19:11-16).

Who Do You Say That He Is?

"Now when Jesus came into the district of Caesarea Philippi, he asked his disciples, '**Who do people say that the Son of Man is?**' And they said, 'Some say John the Baptist, others say Elijah, and others Jeremiah or one of the prophets.' He said to them, '**But who do you say that I am?**' Simon Peter replied, '**You are the Christ, the Son of the living God.**' And Jesus answered him, 'Blessed are you, Simon Bar-Jonah! For flesh and blood has not revealed this to you, but my Father who is in heaven'" (Matthew 16:13-17).

Jesus asked, "Who do people say that I am?" In Jesus time on earth there were many opinions of who Jesus was even as today there are still many opinions. Simon Peter's answer was that Jesus was "the Christ, the Son of the Living God." Jesus is indeed the Son of God who came to earth as the long-awaited Christ who will take the Throne of David and reign forever as King of kings and Lord of lords.

Now Jesus is asking you, "Who do <u>you</u> think that I am?" You have heard the good news of Jesus' saving work on the cross; you have begun to understand what it means that Jesus is Savior, Lord, and Christ. Are you ready to make a decision to personally call on His name? I pray God's Spirit reveals who Jesus is to you so that you believe He is Savior and Lord, and await His return for you as Christ.

At Pentecost, after Jesus ascended into heaven, Peter declared to the people that Jesus, whom they had just crucified, was both Lord and Christ. Based on that sermon, 3000 people believed Jesus was Lord and Christ and cried out, "What shall we do?" Peter's answer was to "Repent!" That will be the subject of the next chapter.

"Let all the house of Israel therefore know for certain that **God has made him both Lord and Christ, this Jesus whom you crucified.**" Now when they heard this they were cut to the heart, and said to Peter and the rest of the apostles, "Brothers, what shall we do?" And Peter said to them, "**Repent and be baptized every one of you in the name of Jesus Christ for the forgiveness of your sins, and you will receive the**

gift of the Holy Spirit. For the promise is for you and for your children and for all who are far off, everyone whom the Lord our God calls to himself" (Acts 2:36-39).

CHAPTER 6 Questions for Thought and Discussion

1. What's in a name...how does this chapter explain what a name represents?

2. "There is power in the name of Jesus" is a common Christian saying. What is the power in each of the names Jesus, Christ, and Lord?

3. a) How do these names have power to meet the needs of your life and heart?

   b) How do these names defeat Satan's work in your life?

4. How did Jesus' life on this earth prove that He has earned and deserves each of these three titles?

5. What difference does it make to you now that Jesus Christ is coming back to earth in the near future to take you to an eternity of glory with Him?

6. Are you ready to bow your knee and confess that Jesus Christ is Lord?

   "Therefore, God has highly exalted him and bestowed on him the name that is above every name, so that **at the name of Jesus every knee should bow**, in heaven and on earth and under the earth, **and every tongue confess that Jesus Christ is Lord**, to the glory of God the Father" (Philippians 2:9-11)

CHAPTER 7

Going Jesus' Way

"Then I saw a great white throne and him who was seated on it. From his presence earth and sky fled away, and no place was found for them. And I saw the dead, great and small, standing before the throne, and books were opened. Then another book was opened, which is the book of life. And **the dead were judged by what was written in the books, according to what they had done.** And the sea gave up the dead who were in it, Death and Hades gave up the dead who were in them, and **they were judged, each one of them, according to what they had done.** Then Death and Hades were thrown into the lake of fire. This is the second death, the lake of fire. And **if anyone's name was not found written in the book of life,** he was thrown into the lake of fire." (Revelation 20:11-15).

The final thing that we need to talk about in more depth is that after Jesus returns to earth as King of kings and Lord of lords, there will be a day of judgment when all people "great and small" will be judged. "It is appointed for man to die once, and after that comes judgment" (Hebrews 9:27). We will be judged for two things. The first judgment will be if our name is found in the Book of Life or not. If it is found in the Book of Life, it means that we have already made Jesus our Savior and Lord. There are only two kinds of people; those who have Jesus as their Savior and Lord and thereby have life and will be saved, and those who do not have Jesus, who do not have life and will not be saved.

"And this is the testimony, that God gave us eternal life, and this life is in his Son. **Whoever has the Son has life; whoever does not have the Son of God does not have life**" (1 John 5:11-12).

"For everyone who calls on the name of the Lord will be saved" (Romans 10:13).

Those whose names are <u>not</u> found in the Book of Life will be "thrown into the lake of fire" to be punished for eternity. They will be punished because they did not accept the gospel or good news of who Jesus is and what He has done for them on the cross. They did not give their sins to Jesus, who was willing to take their punishment when He went to the cross. Without Jesus, they will have to receive the punishment for sin themselves because God is a righteous God who demands justice.

"When the Lord Jesus is revealed from heaven with his mighty angels in flaming fire, **inflicting vengeance on those who do not know God and on those who do not obey the gospel of our Lord Jesus**. They will suffer the punishment of eternal destruction, away from the presence of the Lord and from the glory of his might" (2 Thessalonians 1:7-9).

God's justice is a good thing. Finally, all those who have not repented of their sins and received Jesus as their Savior, who are responsible for all the injustice in the world like child abuse, sexual abuse, human trafficking, murder, lying, greed, embezzlement, and the misappropriation of the world's resources, etc. will receive justice. God is a just God and has noticed every sin of injustice. He has taken notice of every sin that has not been righted against us that we thought would never be avenged. He will right all wrongs. At the same time, it means that each of us must take this opportunity on the earth to repent of the sin in our own life before justice is served on the last day and we receive the punishment of eternal destruction away from the presence of God.

In the second judgment, each of us will be judged for what we have done during our lives on earth and rewarded accordingly. The unrepentant people's sins will be judged and the appropriate punishment meted out; while the believers will be rewarded for the good that they have done while on earth.

"For the Son of Man is going to come with his angels in the glory of his Father, and then **he will repay each person according to what he has done**" (Matthew 16:27).

"**He will render to each one according to his works**: to those who by patience in well-doing seek for glory and honor and immortality, he will give eternal life; but for those who are self-seeking and do not obey the truth, but obey unrighteousness, there will be wrath and fury" (Romans 2:6-7).

"For we will all stand before the judgment seat of God; for it is written, "As I live, says the Lord, every knee shall bow to me, and every tongue shall confess to God." So, then **each of us will give an account of himself to God**" (Romans 14:10, 12).

"**Each one's work will become manifest**, for the Day will disclose it, because it will be revealed by fire, and the fire will test what sort of work each one has done. If the work that anyone has built on the foundation survives, **he will receive a reward**. If anyone's work is burned up, he will suffer loss, though he himself will be saved, but only as through fire" (1 Corinthians 3:13-15).

"For we must all appear before the judgment seat of Christ, so that **each one may receive what is due for what he has done in the body, whether good or evil**" (2 Corinthians 5:10).

"Then the seventh angel blew his trumpet, and there were loud voices in heaven, saying, "The kingdom of the world has become the kingdom of our Lord and of his Christ, and he shall reign forever and ever." And the twenty-four elders who sit on their thrones before God fell on their faces and worshiped God, saying, "We give thanks to you, Lord God Almighty, who is and who was, for you have taken your great power and begun to reign. The nations raged, but your wrath came, and **the time for the dead to be judged, and for rewarding your servants, the prophets and saints, and those who fear your name, both small and great,** and for destroying the destroyers of the earth" (Revelation 11:15-18).

Good works will not be the basis as to whether they are saved because good works do not "justify" us. "Justify" means to make us right in God's eyes. Only the blood of Jesus can justify us. Our good works do not outweigh our bad deeds. God's demand for righteousness cannot be appeased with human works. He demands a righteousness that only Jesus in His sinless state could fulfill. Our salvation is not based on our good works but is a free gift of God's grace. "Grace" means a free gift of God's unearned favor. God's grace is a gift of undeserved favor, in giving Jesus Christ to die on the cross to save us and secure eternal life with God for us.

"**For by works of the law no human being will be justified in his sight**" (Romans 3:20).

"For by grace you have been **saved through faith**. And this is not your own doing; it is the gift of God, **not a result of works**, so that no one may boast" (Ephesians 2:8-9).

"He saved us, **not because of works done by us** in righteousness, but according to his own mercy" (Titus 3:5).

What does it mean to be "saved by faith" in Ephesians 2:8? Faith is truly more than only agreeing with our mind, because even demons know with their head that Jesus is God, yet shudder (see James 2:19). Cognitive assent is part of a decision to make Jesus Savior and Lord, but it must also involve our whole life. God said in the Old Testament, and Jesus quoted from that, saying, "You shall love the Lord your God with all your heart and with all your soul and with all your strength and with all your mind" (Luke 10:27). Our response to God must be with our whole life: with all of our emotions, desires, energy, and thoughts, which will affect all the actions of our body. It will affect every decision we make. It will change our life! It means exchanging our sinful life for the new life Jesus offers us through His death and resurrection. It means changing the whole direction of our life from going our own way to following Jesus as our Savior and Lord.

The Bible says "Faith is the assurance of things hoped for, the conviction of things not seen" (Hebrews 11:1). When we walk by faith, we do not walk by sight (see 2 Corinthians 5:7). There is always an element of faith involved in making a decision to respond to Jesus because we cannot see Him, nor can we scientifically prove this God who is asking us to give our life to Him. It takes a step of faith but we can begin to feel the assurance of what we hope for and the conviction that He is there, even though we can't see God. We need only be willing to take that step of faith and God will confirm it. Jesus once said, "If anyone's will is to do God's will, he will know whether the teaching is from God or whether I am speaking on my own authority" (John 7:17). Once we take that step of faith, the Spirit of God is quick to put a testimony in us that Jesus Christ truly is the Son of God come in the flesh to save us from our sins and that we are His children.

"Whoever believes in the Son of God has the testimony in himself" (1 John 5:10).

"The Spirit himself bears witness with our spirit that we are children of God" (Romans 8:14-16).

"God has sent the Spirit of his Son into our hearts, crying, 'Abba! Father!'" (Galatians 4:6).

How to Make Jesus Savior and Lord

"Let all the house of Israel therefore know for certain that God has made him both Lord and Christ, this Jesus whom you crucified." Now when they heard this they were cut to the heart, and said to Peter and the rest of the apostles, "Brothers, what shall we do?" And Peter said to them, "**Repent** and be baptized every one of you in the name of Jesus Christ for the forgiveness of your sin" (Acts 2:36-39).

In Acts 2, the apostle Peter is preaching, and 3000 people were convinced that Jesus was indeed the Messiah Christ they had been waiting for. They were cut to the heart and asked what they should do. Peter answered that they needed to "repent." "Repent" means to feel and confess sincere regret or remorse about our wrongdoing or sin and make a decision to go the other direction. It literally means to "turn" or "return," or to "change your mind or purpose." In this case, it means to turn from our sin and going our own way, to going God's way. When we repent before God in prayer, our sins are forgiven. We are forgiven by bringing our sins to Jesus so that He can take the punishment that we deserve through His death on the cross, and we can be completely acquitted for all our sins and our sinful condition. In the place of sin, Jesus gives us new life in Himself.

"Thus, it is written, that the Christ should suffer and on the third day rise from the dead, and that **repentance and forgiveness of sins should be proclaimed in his name** to all nations" (Luke 24:46-47).

"**Repent therefore, and turn again, that your sins may be blotted out**, that times of refreshing may come from the presence of the Lord, and that he may send the Christ appointed for you, Jesus" (Acts 3:19).

There are a few facets to the process of repenting and making Jesus your Savior and Lord. Some of these happen at once, in a split second. Some may take time for you to process in your heart but culminate in a change of heart expressed in a prayer to Jesus that only takes a few seconds. Let's look at the four facets of repenting and putting your faith in Jesus Christ as your Savior and Lord that we each must engage in.

1. **Confess Sin**

    Admit that you are a sinner and that you have been going your own way. Admit any specific sins God has brought to mind and those you have been feeling guilty about. Admit that you sin all the time so that you can't possibly name every sin. Going your own way involves good things that are not necessarily bad but may not be what God wants for you. Since the foundation of the world, God has a good plan and purpose for your life! You must turn from going your own way and be willing to go God's way, knowing that He loves us and has good planned for you. Ask God to help you be willing to make that change.

    "**For all have sinned** and fall short of the glory of God" (Romans 3:23).

    "The fool says in his heart, "There is no God." They are corrupt, doing abominable iniquity; there is none who does good. God looks down from heaven on the children of man to see if there are any who understand, who seek after God. **They have all fallen away; together they have become corrupt; there is none who does good, not even one**" (Psalm 53:1-3).

    "If we say we have no sin, we deceive ourselves, and the truth is not in us. **If we confess our sins, he is faithful and just to forgive us our sins and to cleanse us from all unrighteousness**" (1 John 1:8-9).

    "**All we like sheep have gone astray; we have turned—every one—to his own way;** and the LORD has laid on him the iniquity of us all" (Isaiah 53:6).

2. **Have Godly Sorrow**

    Have Godly sorrow or remorse for your sin. If you are truly repentant for your sin and going your own way, you will feel sorry for grieving God as you have sinned against Him and have contributed to Jesus' suffering on the cross. Often you will feel remorse for sinning and going your own way because it has cost you dearly as you have hurt yourself and other people.

"For **godly grief produces a repentance** that leads to salvation without regret, whereas worldly grief produces death" (2 Corinthians 7:10).

3. **Ask to Be Forgiven**

   Ask Jesus to take the punishment for your sin so you don't have to. Acknowledge that you are helpless to help yourself but that you are putting all your hope in Jesus, who took your punishment by dying on the cross in your place. Identify with Jesus on the cross by desiring to be dead to your sin and alive to a resurrected new life in Jesus.

   "And you, who were dead in your trespasses and the uncircumcision of your flesh, God made alive together with him, **having forgiven us all our trespasses, by canceling the record of debt that stood against us with its legal demands. This he set aside, nailing it to the cross**" (Colossians 2:13-14).

4. **Invite Jesus into Your Heart**

   Invite Jesus into your life as Savior and Lord. As Savior, you are giving Him your sins and asking Him to take them to the cross and forgive you. In place of your sins, Jesus will give you His righteousness. As Lord, it means you are no longer in control, He is and you are giving Him your life to lead! In place of going your own way, you must tell God you will make a decision of your will to go His way. Won't you invite Jesus's Holy Spirit into your heart now to be with you, to change your life, and to fellowship with you?

   "Behold, I stand at the door and knock. If anyone hears my voice and opens the door, **I will come in to him and eat with him, and he with me" (Revelation 3:20).**

   "**I have been crucified with Christ. It is no longer I who live, but Christ who lives in me**. And the life I now live in the flesh I live by faith in the Son of God, who loved me and gave himself for me" (Galatians 2:20).

Sample Prayer:
Heavenly Father, I confess that my entire life I have been living in sin and going my own way. I am deeply sorry for sinning against You in all these ways. I admit that I am helpless to save myself and that my only hope is in Jesus' death on the cross in my place for the forgiveness of my sins. Please forgive my sin and count Jesus' punishment in my place. I invite You, Jesus, into my life as my Savior and Lord. Please

fill me with Your Holy Spirit. I will follow You forever and turn from going my own way. Thank You for saving me from death and giving me new life in Jesus Christ. Amen.

Praise God! The Bible says that your decision to follow Jesus causes great rejoicing in heaven! God is full of joy to have His relationship with you restored! He is happy to have His child back!

> "Just so, I tell you, there will be more joy in heaven over one sinner who repents than over ninety-nine righteous persons who need no repentance" (Luke 15:7).

This is the greatest decision you have ever made. Your life will never be the same. By accepting Jesus as your Savior and Lord, you are forgiven which means you will not only have eternal life with God after you die, but eternal life starts right now, the minute you give your life to Jesus. Jesus has redeemed your life from the pain, suffering, sickness, and problems sin has caused here on the earth. More than that, you have been justified so that He no longer sees your sins, but only sees you robed in the righteousness of Jesus. Your relationship with God as a son or daughter has been reconciled once and for all!

Forgiveness and salvation are the greatest gifts of God, but they are only just the beginning, just the entrance into all the awesome things God has for you. Once you accepted the forgiveness of your sins and invited Christ into your life, your old life was nailed to the cross and died with Jesus and He has given you a new life. Your old life is gone and you have a new life, Christ living His life in you. Now everything is made new, beautiful, and alive!

> "Therefore, if anyone is in Christ, he is a new creation. The old has passed away; behold, the new has come" (2 Corinthians 5:17).

After Jesus is Your Savior and Lord

1. Be assured that God has forgiven you.

If you have confessed your sin, the Bible says that you are forgiven and that God remembers your sins no more.

> "If we confess our sins, he is faithful and just to forgive us our sins and to cleanse us from all unrighteousness" (1 John 1:8-9).

"As far as the east is from the west, so far does he remove our transgressions from us" (Psalm 103:12).

"Come now, let us reason together, says the LORD: though your sins are like scarlet, they shall be as white as snow; though they are red like crimson, they shall become like wool" (Isaiah 1:18).

"I, I am he who blots out your transgressions for my own sake, and I will not remember your sins" (Isaiah 43:25).

"He will again have compassion on us; he will tread our iniquities underfoot. You will cast all our sins into the depths of the sea" (Micah 7:19).

2. Be assured of your salvation.

If you have invited Jesus into your life, you are saved because "He who has the Son has life!" God wants you to <u>know</u> that you have eternal life. Believe it, it's true!

"But to all who did receive him, who believed in his name, he gave the right to become children of God" (John 1:12).

"Truly, truly, I say to you, whoever hears my word and believes him who sent me has eternal life. He does not come into judgment, but has passed from death to life" (John 5:24).

"God gave us eternal life, and this life is in his Son. Whoever has the Son has life; whoever does not have the Son of God does not have life. I write these things to you who believe in the name of the Son of God **that you may know** that you have eternal life" (1 John 5:10-13).

3. Confess out loud.

Confess out loud that Jesus is your Savior and Lord. Tell somebody about the decision you have made. Find other Christians to fellowship with and tell them about your new decision to follow Christ Jesus.

"If you confess with your mouth that Jesus is Lord and believe in your heart that God raised him from the dead, you will be saved. For with the heart, one believes and is justified, and with the mouth one confesses and is saved. For the Scripture says, "Everyone who believes in him will not be put to shame … For everyone who calls on the name of the Lord will be saved" (Romans 10:9-10).

4. Change Directions.

Having made Jesus Lord by declaring that you are willing to give up going your own way, now begin going Jesus' way and obeying Him with every little decision in life. Desire in your heart to stop sinning in the ways you are aware of. Confess any sin that God brings to mind, turn and begin going God's direction. Obey the Holy Spirit's prompting as you make the necessary changes in your life and circumstances to come into obedience to Christ. Cooperate with God as He works in your life to change you and to give you new life through His Spirit living in you.

> "If you love me, you will keep my commandments…Whoever has my commandments and keeps them, he it is who loves me. And he who loves me will be loved by my Father, and I will love him and manifest myself to him" (John 14:15, 21).

> "Let not sin therefore reign in your mortal body, to make you obey its passions. Do not present your members to sin as instruments for unrighteousness, but present yourselves to God as those who have been brought from death to life, and your members to God as instruments for righteousness" (Romans 6:12-13).

> "And he [*Jesus*] said to all, "If anyone would come after me, let him deny himself and take up his cross daily and follow me. For whoever would save his life will lose it, but whoever loses his life for my sake will save it. For what does it profit a man if he gains the whole world and loses or forfeits himself?" (Luke 9:23-25)

This new life with God is so awesome; no one would ever want their old life back!!! Therefore, it is easy to give up your old life, to give up going your own way, and to begin going God's way. God's way is life and peace and joy! His commands are not burdensome! They become a joy to follow because we know they are a blessing for our good. We are glad to be able to glorify God with our life in response to all the great awesome things He has done for us!

> "For this is the love of God, that we keep his commandments. And his commandments are not burdensome" (1 John 5:3).

"This God--his way is perfect; the word of the LORD proves true; he is a shield for all those who take refuge in him" (Psalm 18:30).

"Your way, O God, is holy. What god is great like our God?" (Psalm 77:13)
"Blessed are those whose way is blameless, who walk in the law of the LORD! Blessed are those who keep his testimonies, who seek him with their whole heart, who also do no wrong, but walk in his ways!" (Psalm 119:1-3)

Since God loved you so much to send Jesus to die for you, there is no limit to the love that He will lavish on you and the good things He promises to give you. He is able to give you abundantly more than you could even think to ask for! He promises you an abundant life in Him.

"What then shall we say to these things? If God is for us, who can be against us? He who did not spare his own Son but gave him up for us all, how will he not also with him graciously give us all things?" (Romans 8:31-32)

"Now to him who is able to do far more abundantly than all that we ask or think, according to the power at work within us" (Ephesians 3:20).

"I came that they may have life and have it abundantly" (John 10:10).

There is so much to learn and experience in going God's way that it will take your whole life to understand, receive, apply and grow into the full potential that God has in store for you. And this is just the beginning; in eternity He offers us so much more that our minds can't even comprehend it now! The next three chapters will help you better understand three of the things that have transpired in your decision to follow Jesus: your old life is gone and you have been given new life, you have been filled with the Holy Spirit, and you have been transferred from the kingdom of darkness into the Kingdom of Jesus Christ!

"Make me to know your ways, O LORD; teach me your paths. Lead me in your truth and teach me, for you are the God of my salvation; for you I wait all the day long" (Psalm 25:4-5).

CHAPTER 7 Questions for Thought and Discussion

1. According to this chapter, what are the two judgments going to be about on judgment day?

2. What is the difference between being sorry for your sin and being repentant of your sin?

3. a) According to the following verse, what are three requirements of a faith that will please God?

   b) Do you have those three aspects of faith to save you?

   "And without faith it is impossible to please him, for whoever would draw near to God must believe that he exists and that he rewards those who seek him" (Hebrews 11:6).

4. a) How is there a difference between making Jesus Savior and making Jesus Lord?   b) How are both really the same thing?

5. a) How can you know 100% for sure that you are forgiven and saved?
b) Which of the verses of Scripture that are sited will you recall in times of doubt?

6. a) If you prayed to receive Jesus and make Him your Savior and Lord, who will you tell?
b) And what is one change that you will make in your life right now?

CHAPTER 8

The Exchanged Life

"Therefore, if anyone is in Christ, he is a new creation. The old has passed away; behold, the new has come" (2 Corinthians 5:17).

When you prayed to make Jesus your Savior and Lord and became a follower of Jesus, willing to go His way, there were so many things that transacted spiritually. As we discussed earlier, a true decision to follow Christ involved and impacted your whole heart, mind, soul, and strength, affecting your entire life. This new life is not an "add on" to life as you knew it. It's not just that you added eternal life in heaven after you die to your current earthly life. It's not that you added another philosophy or ideology to be reconstructed into your old way of thinking. It's not that you added a membership to "Christianity" while you remain, for all practical purposes, unchanged. No, the reality of life in Christ Jesus is that everything has changed. Life as you knew it is over and everything has become new! The new philosophy/ideology that you have embraced goes beyond intellectual assent to the power of God that will impact your whole life. Every facet of your life here on earth will experience "salvation," long before you experience eternal life in heaven. In Christ Jesus, your old life has been exchanged for a new life and you have become a new creation.

You will see the evidence of the exchange right away. A quiet peace and joy will overtake you like you have never experienced before. The aching emptiness inside of you for love and relationship will be filled and you will feel satisfied! For the first time ever, you will be able to read the Bible and understand what it is saying, and you will hunger to read it like never before. All of a sudden, your conscience will come alive and you will notice it when you do things you normally did without thinking—even little things like using foul language and profanity. You will begin to feel guilty about things that haven't bothered you for years. You will notice a change in attitude and values that are not like the old you. You will like things you never liked before and dislike things that used to appeal to you. You will wonder, "What has happened to me? I am so different! How did this happen?" Let's find out how and what has happened by taking this verse apart phrase by phrase and look at the new, different life that has become yours in Christ Jesus.

"If Anyone is in Christ"

What does it mean to be "in Christ?" From God's perspective, upon your decision to receive Christ, you were "in Christ Jesus" when He died on the cross. In Jesus' death on the cross, God counted your sins and the consequences of your sin in the punishment and death Jesus suffered. In the spirit, your life was "in Christ Jesus" when He died and it is as if you died with Him. When you prayed to receive Jesus as your Savior, making a decision to follow Him and go His way, you were coming into agreement with and aligning yourself with Jesus Christ and His death on the cross.

> "Do you not know that all of us who have been baptized into Christ Jesus were baptized into his death? **We were buried therefore with him by baptism into death**, in order that, just as Christ was raised from the dead by the glory of the Father, we too might walk in newness of life. For **if we have been united with him in a death like his, we shall certainly be united with him in a resurrection like his**" (Romans 6:3-5**)**.

It is not incidental that an instrument of death, the cross, is the center focus of Jesus and Christianity. Therefore, when you asked Jesus into your life, you identified with His death on the cross, which means death to your old life: your sins, your sinful lifestyle, and going your own way. You identify with Christ on the cross by being willing to lay down your sin and life at the cross. "In Christ" your old life has died on the cross and you are hidden "in Christ" before God.

> "For you have died, and your life is hidden with Christ in God" (Colossians 3:3).

Now you are "hidden with Christ in God" which means as you stand before God now all God can see of you is Christ Jesus. Since you have died with Christ, your sin is covered by the blood of Christ, and you stand robed in the white garments of Christ's righteousness. Jesus has taken your sin on Himself and has covered you with His righteousness. You are forgiven, free of guilt and shame! The debt you owed has been nailed to the cross, and Jesus has taken your punishment. You are free! Even when you sin in the future, you are covered by Jesus' righteousness because when Jesus died, His blood covered all sin: past, present, and future with His blood. In God's sight, your position is righteous, and that never changes, because it is based on Christ's work on the cross and your decision to follow Him, not based on what you do now or in the future. Even though Jesus had never sinned, He took your sin on Himself. Your old life has been exchanged with Jesus' sinless life and you have become the righteousness of God.

"For our sake he made him to be sin who knew no sin, so **that in him we might become the righteousness of God**" (2 Corinthians 5:21).

"I will greatly rejoice in the LORD; my soul shall exult in my God, for he has clothed me with the garments of salvation; **he has covered me with the robe of righteousness**, as a bridegroom decks himself like a priest with a beautiful headdress, and as a bride adorns herself with her jewels" (Isaiah 61:10).

Jesus' death on the cross also conquered sin, and therefore, sin no longer has the same power over your life when you surrender it to Jesus. This means you have power to change whereas before you felt powerless in your battle against sin. The power of sin no longer has power over you to do its bidding. Now "in Christ," based on the victory of the cross over sin, you are no longer a slave to sin but can be set free from it. It means that all the ways you were defeated in your old life, now in Christ you can live victoriously. One by one sins, failures, and weaknesses can be brought to God in prayer on the basis of the cross, and you can claim your righteous position in Christ and have the power to live righteously. We have been redeemed from the curse of sin and our falling short of the law.

"We know that our old self was crucified with him in order that the body of sin might be brought to nothing, so **that we would no longer be enslaved to sin**. For one who has died has been **set free from sin**" (Romans 6:6-7).

"Christ redeemed us from the curse of the law by becoming a curse for us—for it is written, "Cursed is everyone who is hanged on a tree" (Galatians 3:13).

Since you are "in Christ's death," you died with Christ and have exchanged your old life for new life "in Christ Jesus." Since you were in His death, you are also in His resurrection and your life has been regenerated even as He rose from the dead. You have been made alive together with Him and now have His abundant life on earth and His eternal life forever. Just as we died with Him, our life can be resurrected with Him to a life full of Jesus—a life full of His love, joy, peace, faith, power, etc. In fact, Jesus wants to live His life through us so that it is no longer us who live but Him who lives in us.

> "Now if we have died with Christ, we believe that we will also live with him" (Romans 6:8).

> "And you, who were dead in your trespasses and the uncircumcision of your flesh, **God made alive together with him,** having forgiven us all our trespasses, by canceling the record of debt that stood against us with its legal demands. This he set aside, nailing it to the cross" (Colossians 2:13-14).

"He is a New Creation"

> "I have been crucified with Christ. It is no longer I who live, but Christ who lives in me. And the life I now live in the flesh I live by faith in the Son of God, who loved me and gave himself for me" (Galatians 2:20).

What makes you a new creation is that the old you is no longer alive; now Christ is living His life in you. You have been crucified with Christ so you are dead to sin and your own way of doing things, which allows Christ room to live through you. If you are in His death, then you are in His resurrection and have His life in you. His Holy Spirit dwelling in you will give life to your human spirit, soul, and body.

> "But if Christ is in you, although the body is dead because of sin, the Spirit is life because of righteousness. If the Spirit of him who raised Jesus from the dead dwells in you, he who raised Christ Jesus from the dead will also give life to your mortal bodies through his Spirit who dwells in you" (Romans 8:10-11).

So, what does it mean that you are "a new creation?" What is new is that Christ is living His life in and through you. According to 2 Corinthians 3, when you turn to the Lord, the veil that blocked the experience and reality of God out of your life has been removed. You have become one with Christ, and His Holy Spirit sets you free to be transformed into the image of Christ in you. This process is the transforming work of the Holy Spirit in us that grows more glorious in us year after year as we come to know Jesus better and better.

> "But when one turns to the Lord, the veil is removed. Now the Lord is the Spirit, and where the Spirit of the Lord is, there is freedom. And we all, with unveiled face, beholding the glory of the Lord, are being **transformed** into the same image from one degree of glory to another. For this comes from the Lord who is the Spirit" (2 Corinthians 3:16-18).

The word in Scripture used for transformed is *"metamorphoo"* from which we get the word metamorphous and means to "change condition" or "to change into another form." In this case, it means inward change that expresses itself in your outward life. When you turn to Christ, and you are in Him and He is in you, an invisible process begins which changes us to conform to the image of Christ in us. As we make room for Him to live His life through us, we appear to be more and more like Him. We exchange our old life and in its place are filled with Jesus' new life.

In God's eyes, your position is in Christ Jesus. Consequently, you are a new creation because He already sees you in the righteousness of Christ Jesus. From our earthly perspective, the Holy Spirit in us begins transforming us to the image of Christ from the minute we receive Him as Savior. Some things are transformed immediately with great ease. These are the things we will notice right away. Some things require us to line up our thinking with the mind of Christ by listening to the Holy Spirit in us and in the written word of God in the Bible so that we understand God's thoughts and how He wants us to live.

> "Do not be conformed to this world, but **be transformed** by the renewal of your mind, that by testing you may discern what is the will of God, what is good and acceptable and perfect" (Romans 12:2).

There are also some things that are entangled or set in strongholds that God will work on over a period of time as we submit them to Him. As we walk with God, He knows the best timing and will reveal things to us as we are ready to be transformed in those areas of our life. These things may require us to look deep in our hearts at sins that need repentance, at pain that we have repressed, at decisions of our will that we need to renounce, and at wrong belief systems that we need to replace with the truth. In the context of a relationship with God, our entire life as a Christian will be a process of transformation and we will become more and more like Jesus, who is in us. Even though in God's eyes you are righteous and your salvation is secure, and becoming a child of God causes a great transformation in our lives, there will always be things we can be praying about and aligning ourselves with the Holy Spirit to allow Jesus more and more freedom to live His life through us. Our old life will be given over to death so that it can be exchanged for the life of Jesus to be manifest in us.

> "For we who live are always being given over to death for Jesus' sake, so that the life of Jesus also may be manifested in our mortal flesh" (2 Corinthians 4:11).

"The Old Has Passed Away"

When you prayed to receive Jesus as your Savior, you embraced the cross for yourself and said, "I am willing to die to my way of life, to the sin I willingly used to commit, and to a lifestyle of going my own way instead of God's way." You may have realized that the price Jesus paid by suffering and dying on the cross for you to be set free from your empty way of living makes Him worthy of giving your whole life to Him. The exchanged life is such that Christ gave up His position in heaven for us to take our punishment, facing death and the devil in our place. Therefore, He is worthy of us giving up our life for Him. We should no longer live for ourselves but for Him who died for us. He is worthy of everything we are, everything we do, everything we have!

> "He died for all, **that those who live might no longer live for themselves but for him** who for their sake died and was raised" (2 Corinthians 5:15).

> "Worthy are you…for you were slain, and by your blood you ransomed people for God from every tribe and language and people and nation… "Worthy is the Lamb who was slain, to receive power and wealth and wisdom and might and honor and glory and blessing!" (Revelation 5:9, 12)

To have Jesus as Savior assumes a willingness to give up your old life and way of doing things to go in His direction. For most of us, this is not a big sacrifice because we had already come to realize that our old life wasn't working for us anyhow. We were already in despair over the fact that our life was full of disappointments, mistakes, broken relationships, sinful habits, lies, addictions, hurts, and pain. We had already realized that we were spiritually bankrupt and miserable, with no way to help ourselves. We knew that we were blind and unable to see the way out of the mess we had created of our lives, and we were all alone, longing for the communion with God that we were created for. Isn't it amazing that Jesus knows full well that our lives were a mess and yet He offers us to come to Him and receive His life? The life we brought to God is exchanged for life in Christ Jesus that makes us rich, clothes us in righteousness, and makes us able to see.

> "For you say, I am rich, I have prospered, and I need nothing, not realizing that you are wretched, pitiable, poor, blind, and naked. I counsel you to buy from me gold refined by fire, so that you may be rich, and white garments so that you may clothe yourself and the shame of your nakedness may not be seen, and salve to anoint your eyes, so that you may see. Behold, I stand at the door and knock. If anyone hears my voice and opens the door, I will come in to him and eat with him, and he with me" (Revelation 3:17-20).

According to this verse, when you realized your neediness and heard the good news of salvation in Jesus Christ, it is that you felt Jesus knocking on the door of your heart and invited Him to come into your life to commune with you. As this verse says, when you invite Him to come in, He will eat with you and you with Him. You will find the communion with God that you have been longing for, and it will satisfy you better than anything else you have ever tried to make your life better. In fact, you will quickly come to realize that the awesomeness of knowing Jesus as Savior and Lord surpasses all other joys in life and meets all the needs you have ever had. The value of everything else pales in comparison to knowing Christ Jesus your Lord, and living in Him.

> "But whatever gain I had, I counted as loss for the sake of Christ. Indeed, **I count everything as loss because of the surpassing worth of knowing Christ Jesus my Lord**. For his sake I have suffered the loss of all things and count them as rubbish, in order that **I may gain Christ and be found in him**" (Philippians 3:7-9).

Paul the Apostle, who wrote these verses, says here that he counted his old life as a loss and as rubbish. He was referring to his life in which he was one of the most successful, elite, ruling-class leaders of the day! Paul was a Roman citizen when Rome ruled over the Jewish people. Paul was also a Jew of the best class, a Pharisee who prided himself on his self-righteous legalism and his leadership in persecuting the Christians of his day. When Paul met Jesus, he gladly gave all this up in order to be named among the persecuted group which had become followers of Christ called Christians ('little Christs'). Christians at the time were the most despised group in society, being persecuted both by Rome and the Jews, who were martyring Christians. Paul gave up a life of luxury and power in order to take on a despised and persecuted life as a Christian because the only thing that mattered to him, and his only focus, was on the greater value of his new life of knowing Christ Jesus his Lord and being found in Him.

There is a famous quote by a missionary named Jim Elliot who said: *"He is no fool who gives what he cannot keep, to gain that which he cannot lose."* It is <u>not</u> foolish to lay down your life with Jesus on the cross, to die to your sin and your own way of living, to count your old life as rubbish because in the end, nothing in your old life will save you and you would have suffer loss of everything for eternity. To give up your old life here on earth now will gain you a new life that you will not lose in eternity. You will gain abundant life in Christ Jesus here on earth . . . a life of love, joy, peace, and power! A life that will fulfill your purpose and destiny as you come back into relationship with the God who created you, called you, and chose you for a destiny in relationship with Him. Whatever your old life was, whatever was to be gained by it, you can count it as a loss compared to the surpassing worth of this new life in Christ Jesus.

Jesus Himself challenges us with the same challenge if we want to come after Him and be His follower. Jesus said we must deny ourselves and take up our cross to follow Him. To "deny our self and take up our cross" is saying exactly what we have been talking about—it means to be willing to die with Christ on the cross, to die to our sin and our own way of doing things.

> "And he said to all, 'If anyone would come after me, let him deny himself and take up his cross daily and follow me. For whoever would save his life will lose it, but whoever loses his life for my sake will save it. For what does it profit a man if he gains the whole world and loses or forfeits himself?'" (Luke 9:23-25)

Jesus warns us that if we aren't willing to die with Him and lose our old life, we will lose it in the end anyhow. Jesus asks, "What profit would it be to gain pleasure, wealth or power of the whole world if you lose your own soul?" Jesus promises that if we willingly deny our life for His sake, and willingly die to our old self with Him on the cross, we will ultimately save our life—He will save your life, for salvation is in Jesus! He will give us new life; the old will pass away and the new will come.

By praying to receive Jesus as Savior and Lord, you agreed to die to your old self and to say "Yes" to new life in Jesus. This life-changing decision must be followed with daily agreements with the Holy Spirit in you to continue to say "no" to the old life and "yes" to the new life as it pertains to individual life issues and circumstances. The Bible tells us to "put off your old self" with our old way of doing things and to "be renewed in our minds" in the knowledge of God and His way of doing things. We must daily pursue God's help in putting on "His new life" or "to put on the new self," alive in Christ Jesus. With decisions of our will, we must agree with the Holy Spirit in us to go Jesus' way rather than our own in every matter of life.

> "Put off your old self, which belongs to your former manner of life and is corrupt through deceitful desires, and to be renewed in the spirit of your minds, and to put on the new self, created after the likeness of God in true righteousness and holiness" (Ephesians 4:22-24).

What passions and desires do we need to agree to crucify and not gratify, with the Holy Spirit's help? The Bible mentions sins that represent our old life which are of our flesh, not of the Spirit. They are the things we all walked in before receiving Jesus as Savior and Lord, which now we have agreed to "put off" in order to "put on the new life," to "walk as children of light" and to "please the Lord." According to the following verses, there is quite a list of things that could be in our old life that God wants us to put off and exchange for new life in Jesus.

> "Put to death therefore what is earthly in you: **sexual immorality, impurity, passion, evil desire, and covetousness, which is idolatry**. On account of these the wrath of God is coming. In these you too once walked, when you were living in them. But now you must put them all away: **anger, wrath, malice, slander, and obscene talk from your mouth. Do not lie to one another,** seeing that you have put off the old self with its practices and have put on the new self, which is being renewed in knowledge after the image of its creator" (Colossians 3:5-10).

> "Now the works of the flesh are evident: **sexual immorality, impurity, sensuality, idolatry, sorcery, enmity, strife, jealousy, fits of anger, rivalries, dissensions, divisions, envy, drunkenness, orgies, and things like these**. I warn you, as I warned you before, that those who do such things will not inherit the kingdom of God" (Galatians 5:19-21).

"Or do you not know that the unrighteous will not inherit the kingdom of God? Do not be deceived: **neither the sexually immoral, nor idolaters, nor adulterers, nor men who practice homosexuality, nor thieves, nor the greedy, nor drunkards, nor revilers, nor swindlers will inherit the kingdom of God**. And such were some of you. But you were washed, you were sanctified, you were justified in the name of the Lord Jesus Christ and by the Spirit of our God" (1 Corinthians 6:9-11).

"For you may be sure of this, that everyone who is **sexually immoral or impure, or who is covetous (that is, an idolater),** has no inheritance in the kingdom of Christ and God. Let no one deceive you with empty words, for because of these things the wrath of God comes upon the sons of disobedience. **Therefore, do not become partners with them; for at one time you were darkness, but now you are light in the Lord**. Walk as children of light (for the fruit of light is found in all that is good and right and true), and try to discern what is pleasing to the Lord. Take no part in the unfruitful works of darkness, but instead expose them" (Ephesians 5:5-11).

"The New Has Come"

"The truth is in Jesus, to **put off your old self**, which belongs to your former manner of life and is corrupt through deceitful desires, and to be renewed in the spirit of your minds, and **to put on the new self**, created after the likeness of God in true righteousness and holiness" (Ephesians 4:22-24).

"Put to death therefore what is earthly in you… In these you too once walked, when you were living in them. But now you must put them all away… seeing that you have **put off the old self with its practices** and have **put on the new self**, which is being renewed in knowledge after the image of its creator" (Colossians 3:5-10).

According to these two verses, when the old self is put off, it is replaced with a new self that is made in the likeness or image of God, in righteousness and holiness. How can that be? How can we become righteous and holy? It can only be possible in that our old life dies and is replaced by the Holy Spirit living in us and that we have become one spirit with Him. "But he who is joined to the Lord becomes one spirit with him" (1 Corinthians 6:17). It is only as we walk by the power of the Holy Spirit in us that new life comes, and that we can turn from living according to the desires of our old life by crucifying the flesh with its passions and desires.

> "But I say, walk by the Spirit, and you will **not gratify the desires of the flesh**. For the desires of the flesh are against the Spirit, and the desires of the Spirit are against the flesh, for these are opposed to each other, to keep you from doing the things you want to do. But if you are led by the Spirit, you are not under the law… For those who live according to the flesh set their minds on the things of the flesh, but those who live according to the Spirit **set their minds on the things of the Spirit**. And those who belong to Christ Jesus have **crucified the flesh with its passions and desires**. If we live by the Spirit, let us also keep in step with the Spirit" (Galatians 5:18-23).

How do we put on the new life? We must set our mind on things of the Spirit rather than things of the flesh. When we received Jesus Christ, His Holy Spirit filled our spirit and gave us the mind of Christ. The Holy Spirit is able to speak right to our thoughts and conform our thinking to the thinking of Christ because we have been given the mind of Christ. "We have the mind of Christ" (1 Corinthians 3:16). However, the majority of the times the Holy Spirit speaks to us is through the context in which we live. God does not generally work in a vacuum but is constantly speaking to us through the things around us. He uses everything and everyone around us to transform us. However, some things are better conductors of the Holy Spirit than others. That means it is necessary to change the context of life around us. If we continue watching the same TV shows and movies, going to the same websites, reading the same magazines and books, hanging out with the same friends, our life will continue to look pretty much the same. When we focus our mind on Jesus, the Holy Spirit is going to have more to work with in order to transform us to new life in Him.

The following four passages give us a clue as to how to put off the old self and put on the new. According to these verses, the way we can participate with God in His transformation of us is to renew our minds. In Romans 8, God talks about setting our mind on things of the Spirit rather than things of the flesh. God says that the mind set on the flesh or the old life is death, but the mind set on the Spirit is life. This means a change in our focus and a change in what we put into our minds. Renewing our mind involves exposing ourselves to godly media, literature and relationships. Most importantly, the more we spend time reading the Bible, which is the written word of God, the more opportunity the Holy Spirit has to work God's mind in us and transform our thinking to the mind of Christ.

> "For those who live according to the flesh **set their minds** on the things of the flesh, but those who live according to the Spirit **set their minds on the things of the Spirit**. For to **set the mind on the flesh is death, but to set the mind on the Spirit is life and peace**. For the mind that is set on the flesh is hostile to God, for it does not submit to God's law; indeed, it cannot. Those who are in the flesh cannot please God" (Romans 8:5-8).

> "Do not be conformed to this world, but **be transformed by the renewal of your mind**, that by testing you may discern what is the will of God, what is good and acceptable and perfect" (Romans 12:2).

> "The truth is in Jesus, to put off your old self, which belongs to your former manner of life and is corrupt through deceitful desires, and to **be renewed in the spirit of your minds**, and to put on the new self, created after the likeness of God in true righteousness and holiness" (Ephesians 4:22-24).

> "Put to death therefore what is earthly in you... In these you too once walked, when you were living in them. But now you must put them all away... seeing that you have put off the old self with its practices and have **put on the new self, which is being renewed in knowledge after the image of its creator**" (Colossians 3:5-10).

As we renew our minds with the truth of God's word, we will see many ways to align our thoughts, will, emotions, and actions with God's way. Our entire Christian life is a process of becoming more and more one with the thoughts and purposes of God in our lives and allowing God to produce the fruit of the Holy Spirit in our lives.

> "But the fruit of the Spirit is love, joy, peace, patience, kindness, goodness, faithfulness, gentleness, self-control; against such things there is no law. And those who belong to Christ Jesus have crucified the flesh with its passions and desires. If we live by the Spirit, let us also keep in step with the Spirit" (Galatians 5:22-25).

New life is released in us as we live by the Spirit and keep in step with the Spirit of God. We live by the Spirit and keep in step with the Spirit by abiding in Christ Jesus. "By this we know that we abide in Him, and He in us, because He has given us of his Spirit" (1 John 4:13). Jesus compared the Christian life to the life of a grapevine and the branch that produces clusters of grapes. He said that as long as the branch abides or remains in the vine, it will bear fruit, but apart from the vine, the branch can do nothing. Bearing good fruit is not something that a branch can do by itself without a vine; it is a natural by-product of remaining in the life of the vine.

> "Abide in me, and I in you. As the branch cannot bear fruit by itself, unless it abides in the vine, neither can you, unless you abide in me. I am the vine; you are the branches. Whoever abides in me and I in him, he it is that bears much fruit, for apart from me you can do nothing" (John 15:4-5).

Likewise, we cannot produce new life by our own effort. New life is a natural product of being in Christ and allowing His Holy Spirit to live His life through us. All that God desires us to do is spend time with Jesus by fixing our mind on Him and being willing to lay down our old life and our own ways to make room for His new life in us. By remaining or abiding in Him, our old life will be exchanged with new life of His Holy Spirit, and the old works of the flesh will be exchanged with the fruit of the Spirit: love, joy, peace, patience, kindness, goodness, faithfulness, gentleness, and self-control.

CHAPTER 8 Questions for Thought and Discussion

1. When Jesus died on the cross, what did He take from you, and what did He give you?

2. a) What does it mean to be "in Christ" from God's perspective?
   b) What are the benefits from your perspective?

3. a) What does it mean for you to have "Christ living in you?"
   b) What are the benefits for you?

4. What "old things" are you thankful are gone, or you are looking forward to letting go of?

5. What "new things" are you looking forward to enjoying "in Christ?"

6. What will you do to practice renewing your mind with the new things of God?

CHAPTER 9

Life in the Holy Spirit

"Be filled with the Spirit" (Ephesians 5:18).

In chapter 6 there was the opportunity to make a dramatic change in your life by choosing to go God's way instead of your own. This huge decision that involves so many facets of transformation happened all at once, and now we are trying to examine what actually occurred, one aspect at a time. One of the most exciting aspects of inviting Jesus Christ into your life is that in that moment His Holy Spirit came into and filled your spirit which is called regeneration. The life of God which was lost by Adam at the "fall of all humans" is regenerated in your spirit and you became one with the Spirit of God again. Your spirit is filled with the Holy Spirit and it has been sealed as a guarantee or down payment of our eternal inheritance in heaven with God.

> "And it is God who establishes us with you in Christ, and has anointed us, and who has also put his seal on us and **given us his Spirit in our hearts** as a guarantee" (2 Corinthians 1:21-22).

> "In him you also, when you heard the word of truth, the gospel of your salvation, and believed in him, were **sealed with the promised Holy Spirit**, who is the guarantee of our inheritance until we acquire possession of it, to the praise of his glory" (Ephesians 1:13-14).

In the last chapter, we talked about how the old life is gone and new life has come. "New life" is a natural product of being in Christ and allowing His Holy Spirit to live His life through us. New life is not produced by our own effort. When we invited Jesus into our life, our flesh or old self didn't get transformed, it died with Christ on the cross. In the new life, we can invite the Holy Spirit to fill our mind, heart and will more and more. It is the Holy Spirit living in us that transforms our heart, mind and will, and makes our life new. It is the Holy Spirit in us that makes it possible for us to think about and understand things with the mind of Christ, to make new choices and carry them out.

So, who is the Holy Spirit? In the Bible, God is described in terms of a Triune God that consists of the Father, Son, and the Holy Spirit. It is beyond the human mind to fully grasp how God works as a Trinity, but we do know from Scripture that it is true. Throughout Scripture, there are times when all three persons are mentioned as being active together. For instance, at Creation, "God created the heavens and the earth" (Genesis 1:1) and "The Spirit of God was hovering over the face of the waters" (Genesis 1:2). It is written of Jesus: "He was in the beginning with God. All things were made through him, and without him was not anything made that was made" (John 1:2-3). Later in creation week, when God was creating man, He spoke of Himself in plural, which supports the idea of a Trinity though He didn't mention it directly: "Then God said, "Let **us** make man in **our** image, after **our** likeness" (Genesis 1:26). Another place where we can see the Trinity in Scripture is at Jesus' baptism.

> "And when **Jesus** was baptized, immediately he went up from the water, and behold, the heavens were opened to him, and he saw **the Spirit of God** descending like a dove and coming to rest on him; and behold, **a voice from heaven said, "This is my beloved Son**, with whom I am well pleased" (Matthew 3:16-17).

In this passage, we see Jesus being baptized by John the Baptist, at the same time the Holy Spirit descends shaped like a dove, and God the Father speaks as a voice from heaven, calling Jesus His Son. Jesus' parting exhortation to His disciples was to baptize "in the name of the Father and of the Son and of the Holy Spirit" (Matthew 28:19). Throughout His time on earth, Jesus referred many times to God as Father and addressed Him as Father in His prayers. Jesus also talked about the Holy Spirit and promised that when He returned to heaven, He would send us His Holy Spirit to be with us forever.

Before Jesus began His public ministry by being baptized, John the Baptist was already watching for Him and was prophesying that one greater than himself would come who would baptize with the Holy Spirit and fire.

> "I baptize you with water for repentance, but he who is coming after me is mightier than I, whose sandals I am not worthy to carry. He will baptize you with the Holy Spirit and fire" (Matthew 3:11).

Even before John the Baptist, the baptism of the Holy Spirit had already been prophesied in the Old Testament. The prophet Joel said that in the last days, God would pour out His Spirit on all flesh, releasing gifts of revelation in the form of prophecy, dreams, and visions. The Holy Spirit has been active on earth since creation and throughout the Old Testament He is spoken of many times. However, the baptism of the Holy Spirit was not given until Jesus came to earth and then returned to heaven. Jesus said that it was better that He would go to heaven so that every one of us could have the Holy Spirit with us.

> "And it shall come to pass afterward, that **I will pour out my Spirit on all flesh**; your sons and your daughters shall prophesy, your old men shall dream dreams, and your young men shall see visions. Even on the male and female servants **in those days I will pour out my Spirit**" (Joel 2:28-29).

> "I tell you the truth: it is to your advantage that I go away, for if I do not go away, the Helper will not come to you. But **if I go, I will send him to you**" (John 16:7).

Right before He ascended into heaven, Jesus asked His disciples to wait in Jerusalem for the promised baptism of the Holy Spirit, upon which they would receive power and would be His witnesses.

> "And while staying with them he ordered them not to depart from Jerusalem, but to wait for the promise of the Father, which, he said, 'you heard from me; for John baptized with water, but you will be baptized with the Holy Spirit not many days from now... But **you will receive power when the Holy Spirit has come upon you, and you will be** my witnesses in Jerusalem and in all Judea and Samaria, and to the end of the earth.' And when he had said these things, as they were looking on, he was lifted up, and a cloud took him out of their sight" (Acts 1:4-9).

And that is exactly what happened. Jesus' disciples were meeting together in Jerusalem, waiting for the baptism of the Holy Spirit. On the 40th day of waiting, on the Jewish Festival of Pentecost, the Holy Spirit suddenly fell on them with tongues of fire and each of them began speaking in a new language. Great passion and courage overtook them and they went into the streets of Jerusalem where thousands of Jews had gathered to celebrate the Pentecost Festival and the disciples began to tell them about Jesus. The miraculous thing is that although the people who had gathered in Jerusalem were from all over the world, the disciples spoke to them in their own languages and 3000 of them became followers of Jesus.

> "When the day of Pentecost arrived, they were all together in one place. And suddenly there came from heaven a sound like a mighty rushing wind, and it filled the entire house where they were sitting. And divided tongues as of fire appeared to them and rested on each one of them. And they were all filled with the Holy Spirit and began to speak in other tongues as the Spirit gave them utterance" (Acts 2:1-4).

On that day, Peter told them that what was happening was the baptism of the Holy Spirit prophesied in Joel. He also boldly preached about Jesus being the Savior and Christ, and told them that if they repented of their sin and identified themselves as followers of Jesus in baptism, they would receive the Holy Spirit. He said that this promise of the Holy Spirit was for them and their children and everyone "far off" who would come after them who would become followers of Jesus Christ, which would include you.

> **"Repent and be baptized every one of you in the name of Jesus** Christ for the forgiveness of your sins, **and you will receive the gift of the Holy Spirit.** For the promise is for you and for your children and for all who are far off, everyone whom the Lord our God calls to himself" (Acts 2:38-39).

At Pentecost, the 3,000 people in the crowd believed in Jesus and immediately received the baptism of the Holy Spirit. Later in the Book of Acts, some people received the Holy Spirit when they were first saved (see Acts 10:44-48; 11:15-16). There were other people who did not hear about the Holy Spirit until sometime after they had been saved, and the Holy Spirit fell on them at that time (see Acts 8:14-17; 9:17; 19:1-6). As one of those "who are far off" and have called on the name of Jesus as your Savior and Lord, you too have received the regeneration of the Holy Spirit at the same time you received Jesus into your life. Being filled with the Holy Spirit is one aspect of the miracle of salvation as explained in Chapter 6: "Invite His Holy Spirit into your heart to be with you, to change your life, and to fellowship with you." If you prayed to become a follower of Jesus long before you read this book, you too have received the Holy Spirit in your spirit and in prayer can welcome the Holy Spirit and invite Him to fill you completely, spirit, soul and body. We can all continue to ask to be refilled and empowered with more of the Holy Spirit. In Greek the verb "be filled" in the verse "Be filled with the Spirit" (Ephesians 5:18) is in the continuous form of the verb, which actually means: "keep being filled" with the Holy Spirit. In Luke 4:1 Jesus was led into the wilderness "full of the Holy Spirit" and in Luke 4:14 came out of the desert "in the power of the Spirit." We can continually ask for the Holy Spirit to fill us more and empower us, as there always is more of us that needs His Spirit.

> "If you then, who are evil, know how to give good gifts to your children, how much more will the heavenly Father give the Holy Spirit to those who ask him" (Luke 11:13).

THREE ROLES OF THE HOLY SPIRIT

Salvation

The first and most important role of the Holy Spirit is to lead us into salvation by 'convicting us of sin and righteousness and judgment.' This began as regeneration of the Holy Spirit when we became believers and will continue until we die. The Holy Spirit's conviction is the only way anyone can come to Christ. It is the Holy Spirit that gives life and no one can come to Jesus without Him.

> "But if I go, I will send him to you. And when he comes, **he will convict the world concerning sin and righteousness and judgment**: concerning sin, because they do not believe in me; concerning righteousness, because I go to the Father, and you will see me no longer; concerning judgment, because the ruler of this world is judged" (John 16:7-11).

> "**It is the Spirit who gives life**; the flesh is no help at all. The words that I have spoken to you are spirit and life. But there are some of you who do not believe." (For Jesus knew from the beginning who those were who did not believe, and who it was who would betray him.) And he said, "This is why I told you that **no one can come to me unless it is granted him by the Father**" (John 6:63-65).

It is the Holy Spirit that actually enables us to become a follower of Christ Jesus. To be born again is a work of the Holy Spirit because "that which is born of Spirit is spirit." Like the wind which we can't see, the Holy Spirit blows life over us so that we can be spiritually born again. When we hear good news of our salvation and believe in Him, we are filled with the promised Holy Spirit.

"Truly, truly, I say to you, **unless one is born of water and the Spirit, he cannot enter the kingdom of God**. That which is born of the flesh is flesh, and that which is born of the Spirit is spirit. Do not marvel that I said to you, 'You must be born again.' The wind blows where it wishes, and you hear its sound, but you do not know where it comes from or where it goes. **So, it is with everyone who is born of the Spirit**" (John 3:3-8).

"But to all who did receive him, who believed in his name, he gave the right to become children of God, who were **born**, not of blood nor of the will of the flesh nor of the will of man, but **of God**" (John 1:12-13).

The fact that you understand the good news of Jesus, are convicted of your sin, and were able to make a decision to receive Jesus Christ, is a powerful miracle of the Holy Spirit for the true message of the Kingdom of God "does not consist in talk but in power" (1 Corinthians 4:20). We are warned to avoid people that have a form of godliness or religion without the power of the Holy Spirit (see 2 Timothy 3:5) for if words are truly from God, they have the power of the Holy Spirit. The Holy Spirit empowers the words that are written or spoken by God to bring conviction and revelation to our hearts and to change lives.

"For we know, brothers loved by God, that he has chosen you, because our gospel came to you not only in word, but also **in power and in the Holy Spirit and with full conviction**" (1 Thessalonians 1:4-5).

"For I decided to know nothing among you except Jesus Christ and him crucified... and my speech and my message were not in plausible words of wisdom, but **in demonstration of the Spirit and of power**, so that your faith might not rest in the wisdom of men but in the power of God" (1 Corinthians 2:2-5).

The written word of God in the Bible is inspired and powerful because the Holy Spirit empowers it. Because of the Holy Spirit, the written word and the good news of the Gospel convicts and impacts our lives. The written word of God in the Bible, comes in power to change hearts; when it is connected with the Spirit to bring life. Ever since Jesus ascended into heaven, the Holy Spirit has been confirming the written word of God that with miracles of salvation, transformation, and changed lives. Our lives will transform as we read and study the Bible every day.

"So, then the Lord Jesus, after he had spoken to them, was taken up into heaven and sat down at the right hand of God. And they went out and preached everywhere, while the Lord worked with them and **confirmed the message by accompanying signs**" (Mark 16:19-20).

"For I will not venture to speak of anything except what Christ has accomplished through me to bring the Gentiles to obedience—by word and deed, **by the power of signs and wonders, by the power of the Spirit of God**" (Romans 15:18-19).

"How shall we escape if we neglect such a great salvation? It was declared at first by the Lord, and it was attested to us by those who heard, while **God also bore witness by signs and wonders and various miracles and by gifts of the Holy Spirit distributed according to his will**" (Hebrews 2:3-5).

Connect Us to Jesus

The second most important role of the Holy Spirit after we have been saved is to connect us with Jesus and keep us connected with Jesus. The Holy Spirit is the "Helper." He helps us by bringing to remembrance all that Jesus has told us as recorded in the Bible, He bears witness to us about who Jesus is and what Jesus has revealing about Himself. He glorifies Jesus by revealing Jesus to us. His job is to bring Jesus glory by helping us to know and understand more of Jesus so that we can glorify Jesus better. Jesus also promised that the Holy Spirit will guide us in all truth through the verses of Scripture. If we want to know truth, we will find it in the Scripture.

"But the Helper, the Holy Spirit, whom the Father will send in my name, he will teach you all things and **bring to your remembrance all that I have said to you**" (John 14:26).

"But when the Helper comes, whom I will send to you from the Father, the Spirit of truth, who proceeds from the Father, **he will bear witness about me**" (John 15:26).

"I still have many things to say to you, but you cannot bear them now. When the Spirit of truth comes, **he will guide you into all the truth, for he will not speak on his own authority, but whatever he hears he**

will speak, and he will declare to you the things that are to come. **He will glorify me, for he will take what is mine and declare it to you**. All that the Father has is mine; therefore, I said that he will take what is mine and declare it to you" (John 16:12-15).

Jesus and the Holy Spirit have been with God throughout all of eternity. However, each of the three parts of the Trinity has unique roles that have been active in different ways at different times of human history. God the Father revealed Himself in the Old Testament in many ways, a few of which are: Adonai, (Lord), El Eyon (God Most High and Possessor of Heaven and Earth), and El Shadai (God All-Powerful and All Sufficient). This is how the people of Israel knew God the Father and how we can know Him today. They also knew that a Savior Messiah/Christ was coming, which they were looking forward to. Jesus' life and death on earth proved He was the Messiah. When Jesus came, His role was to live on this earth to reveal God the Father in a visual form that humankind could understand and connect to. "He [Jesus] is the radiance of the glory of God and the exact imprint of his nature" and "the image of the invisible God" (Hebrews 1:3; Colossians 1:15). Jesus said,

> "**Whoever has seen me has seen the Father**. How can you say, 'Show us the Father'? Do you not believe that I am in the Father and the Father is in me? The words that I say to you I do not speak on my own authority, but the Father who dwells in me does his works. Believe me that I am in the Father and the Father is in me, or else believe on account of the works themselves" (John 14:9-11).

Jesus also lived as a perfect human in our place, took our punishment by dying on the cross, conquered death by rising from the dead, and then ascended into heaven where He sits on His throne at the right hand of God the Father. Jesus accomplished His role of salvation on the cross, announcing, "It is finished." Forty days after he ascended to heaven, He sent the Holy Spirit to earth to fulfill the current role of the Spirit on the earth, which is to fill us and connect us to Jesus and the Father. The Holy Spirit in us connects us to the work of salvation that Jesus accomplished on the cross 2,000 years ago. It is the Holy Spirit that enables us to appropriate all the works of the cross: forgiveness, redemption, reconciliation, transformation, victory over death and the devil—they were all made possible by Jesus' death on the cross and His resurrection, but they are all appropriated today by the power of the Holy Spirit. It is the work and role of the Holy Spirit to bring you all the blessings of Jesus death on the cross!

To Be with Us

The third teaching about the Holy Spirit by Jesus was that Jesus would have to leave the earth and would no longer be seen, but in His place, He would send the Holy Spirit who would be in us and with each one of us so that we will not be left alone. He promised not to leave us like orphans (see John 14:19). He has also promised to "never to leave us nor forsake us" (Hebrews 13:5) but to come to us and live in us. The Holy Spirit is the very presence of God in us! Once you surrender your life to Jesus, you experience the very presence of God in your life in the form of the Holy Spirit. Nothing is more glorious than being in the presence of God! Jesus said that having the Holy Spirit in each one of us believers would be better than having the human form of Him on the earth. Jesus promised the Holy Spirit that which would be given to us would be like streams of living waters to refresh our spirit, keep us from thirsting spiritually, and to give us life in Him.

> "Jesus stood up and cried out, 'If anyone thirsts, let him come to me and drink. Whoever believes in me, as the Scripture has said, **'Out of his heart will flow rivers of living water.' Now this he said about the Spirit,** whom those who believed in him were to receive, for as yet the Spirit had not been given, because Jesus was not yet glorified'" (John 7:38-39).

> "I will ask the Father, and **he will give you another Helper, to be with you forever, even the Spirit of truth**... I will not leave you as orphans; I will come to you. Yet a little while and the world will see me no more, but you will see me. Because I live, you also will live. In that day you will know that I am in my Father, and you in me, and I in you" (John 14:16-19).

> "I tell you the truth: it is to your advantage that I go away, for **if I do not go away, the Helper will not come to you. But if I go, I will send him to you**" (John 16:7).

Naturally, when we as a follower of Jesus are filled with the Holy Spirit connecting us with God the Father and Jesus, there are amazing things that happen!! For the Holy Spirit is Himself the presence of God in us! Therefore, there will be amazing manifestations of God's presence in us that manifest the very life of Jesus.

MANIFESTATIONS OF THE SPIRIT

Glorify Jesus

Notice from the roles of the Holy Spirit that His job is always to focus us on Jesus, teach us about Jesus, relay words from Jesus to us, and connect us to Jesus—all in order to glorify Jesus. It is all about Jesus! The Holy Spirit does not glorify Himself nor does He glorify the human whom He fills, nor the church or program. He does not focus on the miraculous, or on angels or demons. The evidence that it is the Holy Spirit in your life and by which you can discern other believer's lives or teaching is that all the focus will be on Jesus; Jesus will get all the glory, all the praise, all the attention. The Apostle Paul said:

> "For Jews demand signs and Greeks seek wisdom, but **we preach Christ crucified**, a stumbling block to Jews and folly to Gentiles" (1 Corinthians 1:23).

> "For **I decided to know nothing among you except Jesus Christ and him crucified**" (1 Corinthians 2:2).

> "For what **we proclaim is not ourselves, but Jesus Christ as Lord**, with ourselves as your servants for Jesus' sake" (2 Corinthians 4:5).

Mind of Christ

The second evidence of the Holy Spirit in your life is that you will have the mind of Christ. It is the Holy Spirit that renews your mind (Ephesians 4:23). Before you came to Christ and were filled with the Holy Spirit, it was impossible to discern spiritual things. Now the Holy Spirit in you will "teach you all things and bring to your remembrance all that Jesus said" (John 14:26). You will be able to hear the voice of the Holy Spirit in your heart and mind; and you will be able to understand the things you hear because the Holy Spirit will give you the understanding. You will be able to understand the written word of God in the Bible and the word of God will be life to your soul.

> "Now we have received not the spirit of the world, but the Spirit who is from God, that we might understand the things freely given us by God. And we impart this in words not taught by human wisdom but taught by the Spirit, interpreting spiritual truths to those who are

spiritual. The natural person does not accept the things of the Spirit of God, for they are folly to him, and he is not able to understand them because they are spiritually discerned… "For who has understood the mind of the Lord so as to instruct him?" But **we have the mind of Christ**" (1 Corinthians 2:12-14, 16).

Fruit of the Spirit

The Holy Spirit in us will transform us to have the character of Jesus. The "fruit of the Spirit" really is the character qualities of Jesus that are not possible to sustain without the help of the Holy Spirit. "The fruit of the Spirit is love, joy, peace, patience, kindness, goodness, faithfulness, gentleness, self-control" (Galatians 5:22). When we are filled with the Holy Spirit, these qualities will be continually increasing in our lives as we deny our flesh and live by the Holy Spirit. We will grow in making choices in our lifestyle to conform to Jesus in us and keep us in step with what the Holy Spirit is doing in our lives. The fruit of a tree is the natural by-product of the tree being rooted and grounded in good soil and water. We will bear fruit as we are rooted and grounded in the Holy Spirit.

"But **the fruit of the Spirit is love, joy, peace, patience, kindness, goodness, faithfulness, gentleness, self-control**; against such things there is no law. And those who belong to Christ Jesus have crucified the flesh with its passions and desires. If we live by the Spirit, let us also keep in step with the Spirit" (Galatians 5:22-25).

Gifts of the Spirit

Besides the fruit of the Spirit, there are the gifts of the Holy Spirit which are a variety of supernatural gifts, ministries, powers, and manifestations that the Holy Spirit works in us to glorify Jesus and minister to the people around us. It is the Holy Spirit who manifests Himself through the gifts "as He wills," giving to each believer as He deems best. Each believer has been given their unique gift set in which they can operate at any time, and there are also different manifestations of the Spirit which are given at specific times as needed. All believers experience these. We may be gifted to teach, serve, give, encourage, shepherd, or administrate (just to name a few) which enables us to minister to others any time we choose within our gifting. Then there are other special times when we see someone healed because of our prayer, or we have a word of encouragement or comfort for someone just when they needed it, to give just a few examples. There are many supernatural manifestations of the Holy Spirit that He longs to work in and through us. We can grow in the gifts of the Spirit as we continue to seek to be filled with the Holy Spirit and step out in faith to practice the gifts we have been given. We are exhorted in 1 Timothy 4:14 not to neglect the spiritual gifts which are given us.

> "Now there are varieties of gifts, but the same Spirit; and there are varieties of service, but the same Lord; and there are varieties of activities, but it is the same God who empowers them all in everyone. To each is given the manifestation of the Spirit for the common good. For to one is given through the Spirit the utterance of wisdom, and to another the utterance of knowledge according to the same Spirit, to another faith by the same Spirit, to another gifts of healing by the one Spirit, to another the working of miracles, to another prophecy, to another the ability to distinguish between spirits, to another various kinds of tongues, to another the interpretation of tongues. All these are empowered by one and the same Spirit, who apportions to each one individually as he wills" (1 Corinthians 12:4-11).

Love

1 Corinthians 13 is all about love. This love chapter has been strategically placed by God right between Chapter 12, which is about the gifts of the Spirit, and Chapter 14, which is about the spiritual gift of tongues. This is significant! It places love as a topic related to the Holy Spirit and states that love is more important than speaking in other tongues or the various gifts. Love is the main evidence of the Holy Spirit. God is love. Jesus proved His love for us by laying down His life for us. It makes sense that the foremost manifestation of the Spirit of God is love. Without love, the gifts of the Spirit mean nothing. Without love, there is no evidence of the Holy Spirit.

> "If I speak in the tongues of men and of angels, but have not love, I am a noisy gong or a clanging cymbal. And if I have prophetic powers, and understand all mysteries and all knowledge, and if I have all faith, so as to remove mountains, but have not love, I am nothing. If I give away all I have, and if I deliver up my body to be burned, but have not love, I gain nothing" (1 Corinthians 13:1-3).

Don't be Deceived

Manifestations of power, whether they are prophecies, healings, or signs and wonders, are not always evidence of the Holy Spirit. The devil is fully capable of speaking to us, giving prophetic words, and doing signs and wonders that counterfeit the gifts and miracles of God. The Bible warns us to beware of false prophets and says that we can recognize them by their fruit. A person whose ministry produces good fruit will be easy to discern from those who produce bad fruit. Ministries that produce bad fruit can be seen in bad character, lack of love and humility, and sinful lifestyles. Often, they bring attention to themselves rather than Jesus, taking credit for what Jesus has done. They talk a lot about money, and focus on building a large kingdom for themselves. Bad fruit does not have the mind of Christ and will contradict the words written in the Bible. On the other hand, the person whose fruit is good lifts up and exalts Jesus rather than themself or the manifestation of the gifts. The focus will be on Jesus, not on building a ministry or bringing revival. They will value Godly character above spiritual gifts and will exhibit the fruit of the Spirit, especially love and humility. A ministry that produces good fruit will elevate the written word of God above current prophecies and experiences.

> "Beware of false prophets, who come to you in sheep's clothing but inwardly are ravenous wolves. **You will recognize them by their fruits**. Are grapes gathered from thorn bushes, or figs from thistles? So, every healthy tree bears good fruit, but the diseased tree bears bad fruit. A healthy tree cannot bear bad fruit, nor can a diseased tree bear good fruit. Every tree that does not bear good fruit is cut down and thrown into the fire. Thus, you will recognize them by their fruits" (Matthew 7:16-20).

> "Not everyone who says to me, 'Lord, Lord,' **will enter the kingdom of heaven, but the one who does the will of my Father who is in heaven**. On that day many will say to me, 'Lord, Lord, did we not prophesy in your name, and cast out demons in your name, and do many mighty works in your name?' And then will I declare to them, '**I never knew you;** depart from me, you workers of lawlessness'" (Matthew 7:20-23).

The deciding factor, according to Matthew 7, is whether we do God's will and are known by Jesus. Not everyone who says "Lord, Lord" will be known by Jesus as being in relationship with Him. To know God's will and to be known by Jesus comes from spending time in His presence: reading His word, praying and seeking Him. Especially in the end times, Satan has been allowed to release many deceiving spirits. For discernment, it is important to spend time in the presence of God so we are able know the good fruit and true manifestations of the Holy Spirit. It is absolutely essential to study the Bible to be able to discern if a word is consistent with God's word in Scripture. A true word will always be aligned with the truth of Scripture.

In these end times it is also essential to love the truth more than religion or spiritual experiences. God warns us in 2 Thessalonians 2:10 that if people love anything more than they love the truth, they will be open for deception. To be able to discern the truth, it is necessary to spend a lot of time with Jesus and getting to know Him by studying the Bible. The best way to discern what spirit is operating is to discern whether what someone says or does is like Jesus and agrees with the Scriptures.

> "Now the Spirit expressly says that in later times some will depart from the faith by devoting themselves to deceitful spirits and teachings of demons, through the insincerity of liars whose consciences are seared" (1 Timothy 4:1-2).

> "But false prophets also arose among the people, just as there will be false teachers among you, who will secretly bring in destructive heresies, even denying the Master who bought them, bringing upon themselves swift destruction. And many will follow their sensuality, and because of them the way of truth will be blasphemed. And in their greed, they will exploit you with false words. Their condemnation from long ago is not idle, and their destruction is not asleep" (2 Peter 2:1-3).

> "The coming of the lawless one is by the activity of Satan with all power and false signs and wonders, and **with all wicked deception** for those who are perishing, **because they refused to love the truth** and so be saved" (2 Thessalonians 2:9-10).

Another way to discern is to ask "by what power?" or "by what name do you do this?" which was the question asked of Apostle Peter when he had healed the cripple man. His answer was that the healing was in the name of Jesus for "there is no other name under heaven given among men by which we must be saved" (Acts 4:7-12). If Jesus is getting the glory, and the focus is on Him, you can discern that the Spirit is the Holy Spirit.

> "Therefore, I want you to understand that no one speaking in the Spirit of God ever says "Jesus is accursed!" and no one can say 'Jesus is Lord' except in the Holy Spirit" (1 Corinthians 12:3).

Holy Spirit in the End Times

"And it shall come to pass afterward, that **I will pour out my Spirit on all flesh**; your sons and your daughters shall prophesy, your old men shall dream dreams, and your young men shall see visions. Even on the male and female servants in those days I will pour out my Spirit" (Joel 2:28-29).

This Old Testament prophecy was fulfilled the first time at Pentecost 40 days after Jesus ascended into heaven. It will be fulfilled again at the end of the days. In the end times, the darkness will increase on the earth, but it will be outshined by the light of God as the Holy Spirit will be poured out on all believers with increased power and light. As the end of the world approaches, the world appears to be getting darker and more evil; but at the same time the glory of God is arising and will shine on true followers of Jesus, empowering them to live Godly lives, discern deception, and have revelation by the power of the Holy Spirit. The light of Jesus will arise so that the glory of God will be manifest in the darkness and will be seen by the nations.

"In Him was life, and the life was the Light of men. The Light shines in the darkness, and the darkness did not comprehend it" (John 1:4-5).

CHAPTER 9 Questions for Thought and Discussion

1. a) Who is the Holy Spirit?
   b) How is He related to Jesus?

2. What does it mean to be baptized with the Holy Spirit?

3. What evidence of the Holy Spirit can you expect to see in your own life once you are saved?

4. a) Why is love the most important quality of the Holy Spirit?

b) What are other fruits of the Spirit you would like to become a part of your life?

5. What gifts of the Spirit do you think God has given to you?

6. How does the Holy Spirit make the life and works of Jesus a reality in your life right now?

CHAPTER 10

Kingdom Life

"From that time Jesus began to preach, saying, 'Repent, for the kingdom of heaven is at hand'" (Matthew 4:17).

Jesus began His ministry on earth by proclaiming that the Kingdom of God was at hand. The Kingdom of God is where Jesus reigns and He is honored and obeyed. Jesus was directing this proclamation towards Satan, who had gained dominion of the earth since Adam and Eve and the fall of humans. Jesus' mission on earth was to conquer Satan and to regain dominion of the kingdom of this world again for Himself. Jesus accomplished this through His death on the cross and His resurrection, which destroyed the devil with all of his works and ways. Because Satan was defeated when Jesus died on the cross and rose again, Satan no longer has authority or legal rights here on this earth. The reality is that Jesus reigns as victor, King of kings, and Lord of lords over His Kingdom on the earth. He sits in the heavens at the right hand of God the Father with every power and authority under His feet.

> "These are in accordance with the working of the strength of His might which He brought about in Christ, when He raised Him from the dead and **seated Him at His right hand in the heavenly [places,] far above all rule and authority and power and dominion, and every name that is named**, not only in this age but also in the one to come. **And He put all things in subjection under His feet**, and gave Him as head over all things to the church, which is His body, the fullness of Him who fills all in all" (Ephesians 1:19-23).

Because Jesus defeated Satan on the cross, Satan no longer has dominion over the earth. However, even though Jesus has defeated Satan and He is seated in the heavenly realm reigning over all powers and authorities; Satan and his demons are allowed access to the earth and human hearts. We don't see all things subject to Jesus Christ right now because God has given us free will to choose who we will serve, and whether we will go our own way (serving Satan) or choose God's way. On this earth we have the freedom to choose Jesus, which actually gives us a chance to reverse the decision Adam and Eve made to go their own way.

Free will is of huge importance to God because He wants us to choose Him out of love for Him not because we have no choice. For love to prevail, we must have a choice and choose Him willingly. The Kingdom of God is where we choose God's way and where we choose Jesus to reign in our hearts and lives. Jesus declared that through repentance we enter the Kingdom of God. As much as we have repented of our sin, chosen to go God's way instead of our own, and obey Jesus as our Lord, we are participating in the Kingdom of God on the earth.

Finally, as we spoke of earlier, at the end of this age, Jesus Christ will come a second time to the earth. Only this time He will come with all power and glory, and He will reign forever and ever with complete dominion and authority. At that time, there will be no more choice, every knee will bow before Him and every tongue will confess that Jesus Christ is Lord. At that time, Jesus' victory on the cross over Satan will be enforced, and Satan will be completely defeated by Jesus' triumphal return to earth as "King of kings and Lord of lords" (Revelation 19-20).

> "Then comes the end, when He has abolished all rule and all authority and power. **For He must reign until He has put all His enemies under His feet**" (1 Corinthians 15:24-25).

> "Thou has put all things in subjection under his feet. For in subjecting all things to him, He left nothing that is not subject to him. **But now we do not yet see all things subjected to him**" (Hebrews 2:8).

When you chose to receive Jesus as your Savior and go Jesus' way, there was a huge legal transaction that occurred in the spiritual realm:

1) Jesus conquered Satan and Satan's authority over your life was cancelled.
2) You have been transferred from Satan's kingdom of darkness into Jesus' Kingdom of Light.
3) You have been positioned with Jesus in heavenly places.
4) You have become a child and saint of God because you stand in Christ Jesus, righteous before God.
5) You are part of the Kingdom of God on the earth.

In many facets of your faith as a believer and the individual decisions that you must make in life, it is essential that you understand these facts according to the Scriptures. When your decisions are based on the truth and reality of these five facts, you can enforce that victory over Satan in your own life.

The reason it is important for you to know all the facts about what has transacted in your salvation decision is that even though Jesus is victorious over Satan, Satan has yet to admit his defeat. Before you made a decision to follow Jesus and go God's way, Satan's efforts were all invested in keeping you from knowing the truth about Jesus, and the good news of forgiveness and salvation. Now Satan will continue to battle for your soul through lies and deception that says he still has authority on the earth and authority over your life. Now that you are saved, Satan's efforts will switch to keeping you in bondage to sin, doubting your forgiveness and salvation, and defeating you by temptation, past sins, and addictions. From there, he goes on to all kinds of mind games and accusations that are lies based in guilt, shame, condemnation, rejection, or lies that you are abandoned or unloved by God. All lies! They are a smokescreen to cover up his own defeat and your new-found freedom in Christ. That is why it is so important for you to know the truth. The two truths at the end of Chapter 7 were that since you gave your life to Jesus, you are forgiven and you have eternal life—you can be assured of these two truths. The truth in Chapter 8 is that you have been given a new life in Christ and your old life in the flesh is gone. The truth of Chapter 9 is that the Spirit of God lives in you. This chapter will look at five truths about the Kingdom of God in your life.

Truth #1: Jesus Defeated the Devil on the Cross.

The reason that Jesus came to earth was to destroy the devil and his works and to cast him out. When Jesus died, He not only forgave our sins by cancelling our debt and nailing it to the cross, He also disarmed the devil and his demons and put them to open shame, or as Bible states:

> "Now is the judgment of this world; **now will the ruler of this world be cast out**. And I, when I am lifted up from the earth, will draw all people to myself" (John 12:31).

> "**The reason the Son of God appeared was to destroy the works of the devil**" (1 John 3:8).

> "**He disarmed the rulers and authorities and put them to open shame, by triumphing over them in him**" (Colossians 2:15).

In addition, in His death and resurrection, Jesus took back the devil's power over death so that now Jesus holds the keys to Death and Hades.

> "Fear not, I am the first and the last, and the living one. I died, and behold I am alive forevermore, and I have the keys of Death and Hades" (Revelation 1:17).

Therefore, we can be free from the fear of death and free of slavery to Satan. Jesus completely triumphed over death and Satan when he rose from the dead.

> "Since therefore the children share in flesh and blood, he himself likewise partook of the same things, **that through death he might destroy the one who has the power of death, that is, the devil, and deliver all those who through fear of death were subject to lifelong slavery**" (Hebrews 2:14-15).

When Jesus ascended to heaven, He was seated at the right hand of God the Father above all rule, authority, power, dominion, and every name that is named. Every spiritual power is now defeated, is in subjection to Jesus, and has been placed under Jesus' feet. This means that Jesus is in control of this world. Even though it may feel like things are out of control or that Satan is able to do what he wants, ultimately Jesus is in control. Satan must submit to Jesus.

> "The working of his great might that he worked in Christ when he raised him from the dead and **seated him at his right hand in the heavenly places, far above all rule and authority and power and dominion, and above every name that is named, not only in this age but also in the one to come. And he put all things under his feet** and gave him as head over all things to the church, which is his body, the fullness of him who fills all in all" (Ephesians 1: 19-23).

Satan was disarmed and stripped of his power by the cross (see Colossians 2:15). Even though the war has been won and Jesus is victor reigning over Satan and his demons, Satan is still under the delusion that he has a chance to defeat Jesus by engaging us in daily battles. His only recourse is to lie to us and try to get us to believe what he says, so that we live according to the lies instead of the truth. In this way, our life is as defeated by Satan as if he really had power to make it happen. Actually, we are doing it to ourselves by choosing to live the lies instead of the truth. This is again another reason to study the Bible, to know the truth.

Without Jesus' help, many battles have been lost to the enemy. However, when we call on Jesus and enforce the victory of the cross found in these five truths, even the battles will be won. According to the Book of Revelation, Satan is never going to win back his authority or dominion of the world. In the end, Jesus will reign on earth forever and will throw Satan into the Lake of Fire forever where he "will be tormented day and night forever and ever" (Revelation 20:10).

"And Jesus came and said to them, '**All authority in heaven and on earth has been given to me.**'" (Matthew 28:18).

"Jesus Christ, who has gone into heaven and **is at the right hand of God, with angels, authorities, and powers having been subjected to him**" (1 Peter 3:21-22).

Truth # 2: Jesus Transferred You from the Kingdom of Satan to the Kingdom of God.

"He has **delivered us from the domain of darkness and transferred us to the kingdom of his beloved Son,** in whom we have redemption, the forgiveness of sins" (Colossians 1:13-14).

"And this is the judgment: the light has come into the world, and people loved the darkness rather than the light because their works were evil. For everyone who does wicked things hates the light and does not come to the light, lest his works should be exposed. **But whoever does what is true comes to the light, so that it may be clearly seen that his works have been carried out in God**" (John 3:18-21).

"And you were dead in the trespasses and sins in which you once walked, following the course of this world, following the prince of the power of the air, the spirit that is now at work in the sons of disobedience— among whom we all once lived in the passions of our flesh, carrying out the desires of the body and the mind, and were by nature children of wrath, like the rest of mankind. But God, **being rich in mercy, because of the great love with which he loved us, even when we were dead in our trespasses, made us alive together with Christ—by grace you have been saved— and raised us up with him and seated us with him in the heavenly places in Christ Jesus,** so that in the coming ages he might show the immeasurable riches of his grace in kindness toward us in Christ Jesus" (Ephesians 2:1-7).

From the above verses, we see that we were rescued from the kingdom of darkness which is under the power of Satan, "the prince of the power of the air, the spirit that is now at work in the sons of disobedience." Before Jesus saved us, we "lived in the passions of our flesh, carrying out the desires of the body and the mind, and were by nature children of wrath, like the rest of mankind." Where we once followed the prince of the power of the air, Satan, and were children of wrath, we now have redemption and the forgiveness of sins in Jesus Christ. Because of God's great love for us, Jesus defeated the devil on the cross to rescue us and deliver us from the kingdom of darkness and transfer us to the Kingdom of Light, the Kingdom of Jesus. Salvation is actually a spiritual transaction defined by God, transferring us from the kingdom of darkness where we were under the power of Satan to the Kingdom of Light; where we now belong to the Lord Jesus Christ, and in Christ Jesus we are seated with him in the heavenly places.

> "To open their eyes, so **that they may turn from darkness to light and from the power of Satan to God,** that they may receive forgiveness of sins and a place among those who are sanctified by faith in me" (Acts 26:18).

> "The Lord Jesus Christ, who gave himself for our sins **to deliver us from the present evil age**" (Galatians 1:4).

To be a citizen of the Kingdom of Light gains us life in the light. Jesus is life in Himself and His life is the light of the world. The darkness of the kingdom of this world has <u>not</u> overcome the light of Jesus. Jesus' light exposes the darkness, making it visible, which makes it light. Anyone who comes to the light will be transformed by the light; by the power of God. Salvation is a transformation of the light eradicating the darkness in your life. The benefit of living in the light is that the old fears, torment, oppression, and temptations of Satan cannot withstand the light and will either flee or be eliminated. "The old is gone, the new has come" (2 Corinthians 5:17). Jesus is the light of the world.

> "In him [*Jesus*] was life, and the **life was the light of men. The light shines in the darkness, and the darkness has not overcome it**" (John 1:4-5).

"Again, Jesus spoke to them, saying, "I am the light of the world. **Whoever follows me will not walk in darkness, but will have the light of life**" (John 8:12).

"But when **anything is exposed by the light, it becomes visible, for anything that becomes visible is light.** Therefore, it says, 'Awake, O sleeper, and arise from the dead, and Christ will shine on you'" (Ephesians 5:13-14).

Not only did Jesus transfer us from the kingdom of darkness to the Kingdom of Light, removing the darkness engulfing us from the outside, He took the darkness that is inside each one of us and is filling our hearts with His light. As much as we agree with the work of the cross by opening our hearts to Jesus, we can experience the transformation of darkness becoming light within us. As we participate with the Holy Spirit by inviting Him into the deep places of our hearts and souls, He brings light to every dark place we open up to Him in prayer. Before we were saved, we buried (repressed) pain, problems, and sin in the dark places of our souls by a decision of our will. As we use our will to open these places to the light of Jesus, these places will be transformed into light. "Anything that becomes visible is light" (Ephesians 5:15).

"For God, who said, "Let light shine out of darkness," has shone in our hearts **to give the light** of the knowledge of the glory of God in the face of Jesus Christ" (2 Corinthians 4:6).

"For **at one time you were darkness, but now you are light in the Lord**. Walk as children of light (for the fruit of light is found in all that is good and right and true)" (Ephesians 5:8-9).

Truth # 3: Jesus is Seated in Heavenly Places and You Are Seated with Him

"He [God the Father] worked in Christ when he raised him from the dead and seated him at his right hand in the heavenly places, far above all rule and authority and power and dominion, and above every name that is named, not only in this age but also in the one to come. And he [God the Father] **put all things under His [Jesus'] feet and gave Him [Jesus] as head over all things to the church, which is his body, the fullness of him who fills all in all**" (Ephesians 1:20-23).

"But God, being rich in mercy, because of the great love with which he loved us, even when we were dead in our trespasses, made us alive together with Christ—by grace you have been saved and **raised us up with him and seated us with him in the heavenly places in Christ Jesus**" (Ephesians 2:4-6).

When Jesus ascended to the heavenly places, He was seated at the right hand of God the Father above "all rule, authority, power, and dominion." The entire spiritual realm was put under Jesus' feet! The second chapter of Ephesians tells us that we, as followers of Jesus, the body of Christ, have been raised up and seated with Christ in the heavenly places. This positions us with Jesus so that every spiritual power that is under His feet is under our feet. In the spirit realm, we are given Jesus' authority over every rule, authority, power, dominion, and name that is named. Christ's authority in us is confirmed in the following passages.

"If you abide in me, and my words abide in you, **ask whatever you wish, and it will be done for you**" (John 15:6).

"You did not choose me, but I chose you and appointed you that you should go and bear fruit and that your fruit should abide, so that **whatever you ask the Father in my name, he may give it to you**" (John 15:16).

We are Jesus' representatives, who come in His authority, enforcing His wishes on the earth. "Therefore, we are ambassadors for Christ, God making his appeal through us" (2 Corinthians 5:20). It would not be advisable to demand our own will because they would not be backed by His authority, but if we are representing His Kingdom where He reigns, we can enforce His will on the earth which includes the victory of the cross where Satan was defeated. Satan's defeat is definitely consistent with the will of God because Jesus has already completed it.

At times it is necessary to remind ourselves that Jesus conquered Satan on the cross, and that Satan's authority over our lives has been cancelled. This is important because Satan will continue to lie and try to deceive us into believing that he has power and authority over our lives. We must know our position with Christ in the heavenly realms. We have authority in Christ's name to enforce Jesus' victory over Satan on the cross and Jesus' rule and reign in our lives on earth today. If we don't enforce the truth of the cross but believe the lies, Satan will keep pushing us backwards, trying to get us to live the old life even though it is gone, having died with Christ on the cross.

The truth of Jesus has the power to set us free. The Bible tells us that Satan is a murderer and liar (see John 8:44), an accuser that condemns (see Revelation 12:10; Romans 8:1), and is at the root of all fear (see 1 John 4:16-18). Accusations, condemnation, and fear are always from Satan, not of the cross. The truth is that spiritually you are positioned in the heavenly realm with Christ Jesus above all power and authority of Satan.

"So, Jesus said to the Jews who had believed him, **'If you abide in my word, you are truly my disciples, and you will know the truth, and the truth will set you free'**" (John 8:31-32).

"**It was for freedom that Christ set us free**; therefore, keep standing firm and do not be subject again to a yoke of slavery" (Galatians 5:1).

"The Spirit of the Lord is upon Me, because He anointed Me to preach the Gospel to the poor. He has sent me **to proclaim release to the captives**, and recovery of sight to the blind, **to set free those who are oppressed**" (Luke 4:18).

Truth # 4: Defeat the Devil by Knowing the Truth about Who You Are in Christ

One of the most important truths of Scripture is who you are "in Christ Jesus" as we talked about in Chapter 7. Two truths about who you are that are important for living in the Kingdom of God are: 1) You are a child of God and therefore belong to Jesus and Satan has no legal right to you; and 2) You are a saint, set apart for God, righteous in God's eyes because of Jesus' blood covering your life.

As a child of God, you are protected by your heavenly Father, your relationship with God has been secured by Jesus Christ, and you are heir to every spiritual blessing in heavenly places. You are God's child because of His great love for you and His choosing you because He wanted a loving relationship with you. You no longer have to live in fear but can freely call out to God, "Abba! Father!" ("Abba" being a warmer, childlike greeting like "Daddy!")

"But to all who did receive him, who believed in his name, **he gave the right to become children of God**" (John 1:12).

"See what kind of love the Father has given to us, that **we should be called children of God; and so, we are**" (1 John 3:1).

"For all who are led by the Spirit of God are sons of God. **For you did not receive the spirit of slavery to fall back into fear, but you have received the Spirit of adoption as sons, by whom we cry, "Abba! Father!"** The Spirit himself bears witness with our spirit that **we are children of God, and if children, then heirs**—heirs of God and fellow heirs with Christ, provided we suffer with him in order that we may also be glorified with him" (Romans 8:14-17).

"**And because you are sons, God has sent the Spirit of his Son into our hearts, crying, 'Abba! Father!' So, you are no longer a slave, but a son, and if a son, then an heir through God**" (Galatians 4:6-7).

It is important to know that you are an heir of God with all of the blessings that are in heavenly places (see Ephesians 1:3), and that Christ redeemed you from the curse of past generations (see Galatians 3:13). Your bloodline has been exchanged for the blood of Christ Jesus; therefore, there is nothing in your past that Satan can hold you in bondage to or responsible for (1 Peter 1:18). We have been released from all legal obligations from our pre-Christ days that Satan might remind us of. We have been adopted into a new family with God as our Father. We no longer belong to Satan's family, and he has no legal right to us or power over us. This is all the victory of the cross which we must enforce by believing the truth and declaring this truth out loud to ourselves and Satan when necessary.

"Blessed [be] the God and Father of our Lord Jesus Christ, **who has blessed us with every spiritual blessing in the heavenly [places] in Christ**" (Ephesians 1:3).

"**Christ redeemed us from the curse of the Law, having become a curse for us**--for it is written, 'CURSED IS EVERYONE WHO HANGS ON A TREE'" (Galatians 3:13).

"Knowing that **you were not redeemed with perishable things like silver or gold from your futile way of life inherited from your forefathers but with precious blood, as of a lamb unblemished and spotless, the blood of Christ**" (1 Peter 1:18-19).

Secondly, you are a "saint," which means to be "separated from sin, consecrated to God, sacred, holy, and devoted to God." Sainthood is something that God has done for us based on the cross of Christ and our righteous standing in Jesus' righteousness. We do not earn biblical sainthood through good behavior; it has only to do with God's calling on our lives to be in a relationship with Him. To be in a relationship with God would assume being in agreement with what pleases Him, and would look like holiness from an outside perspective. Actually, holy living is a gift of God's mercy and grace as He purifies, or works sanctification in our lives.

"So, then you are no longer strangers and aliens, but **you are fellow citizens with the saints** and members of the household of God" (Ephesians 2:19).

"But **you are a chosen race, a royal priesthood, a holy nation, a people for his own possession**, that you may proclaim the excellencies of him who called you out of darkness into his marvelous light. Once you were not a people, but now you are God's people; once you had not received mercy, but now you have received mercy" (1 Peter 2:9-10).

Satan's main objective in every attack on us is to convince us that we do not belong in this wonderful relationship with God so that we draw back and hide from God. When Satan comes with his lies of guilt, shame, condemnation, and accusations, it is important to know that we are saints, consecrated, set apart and holy to God. In Christ Jesus, we have become the righteousness of God (see 2 Corinthians 5:21). We are clothed with the garments of salvation; He has covered us with His robe of righteousness (see Isaiah 61:10).

"He made Him who knew no sin [to be] sin on our behalf, **so that we might become the righteousness of God in Him**" (2 Corinthians 5:21).

"I will rejoice greatly in the LORD, my soul will exult in my God; For **He has clothed me with garments of salvation, He has wrapped me with a robe of righteousness**, as a bridegroom decks himself with a garland, and as a bride adorns herself with her jewels" (Isaiah 61:10).

In order to withstand the devil's barrage of lies, accusations, and condemnation, which are intended to make us feel guilty, ashamed, afraid, rejected, abandoned, and unloved, we must know the truth about God by studying the Scriptures. If we abide in the word of God, we will be His disciple or follower, and we will know the truth that will set us free. The second challenge is to focus our minds on Jesus and the truth found in the word of God. To take captive every thought and make it obedient to Jesus is a weapon of warfare against Satan and has the power to tear down strongholds and to destroy the devil's arguments that are against the true knowledge of God.

"So, Jesus said to the Jews who had believed in him, "**If you abide in my word,** you are truly my disciples, and you will know the truth, and **the truth will set you free**" (John 8:31-3).

"For **the weapons of our warfare** are not of the flesh but have divine power to destroy strongholds. We destroy arguments and every lofty opinion raised against the knowledge of God, and **take every thought captive to obey Christ**" (2 Corinthians 10:5-6).

Truth # 5: Jesus Reigns on This Earth and His Kingdom Comes When We Do His Will and Obey His Word.

Jesus' Kingdom is where He reigns as Lord. What makes Jesus' Kingdom come, is when He leads and is followed by obedient disciples. In the Lord's Prayer, Jesus prayed "Your kingdom come, Your will be done." By this definition, the Kingdom of God is where God's will is done. God's Kingdom comes where His will is done as it is done in heaven. How is God's will done in heaven? The Bible says that in heaven, the angels "do His word," and "obey His voice." We, as followers of Jesus, have the written word of God in the Bible and we hear the still small voice of His Holy Spirit in our inner man. We are functioning in the Kingdom of God when we hear God's word and obey what He says.

"Our Father in heaven, hallowed be your name. **Your kingdom come, your will be done on earth as it is in heaven**" (Matthew 6:10).

"Bless the LORD, O you his angels, **you mighty ones who do his word, obeying the voice of his word!** Bless the LORD, all his hosts, his ministers, who do his will!" (Psalm 103: 20-21)

The Kingdom coming to earth through obedience to the will of God is true of the big picture on the earth, and it is equally true of your heart. Jesus is Lord and King where He is obeyed and His Kingdom is advanced through obedience to Him. Satan's kingdom is defeated through obedience to Jesus. When we make individual decisions to do God's will, the Kingdom of God will continue to increase in our lives, and we will experience more and more of the victory of Christ Jesus over sin, death, and the devil. In so doing we will advance the Kingdom of God on the earth.

The bottom line of Kingdom living is that to experience the life of God in the Kingdom of God, we must obey His will; therefore, we can take "no part in the unfruitful works of darkness" (Ephesians 5:11). There are many passages in Scripture that exhort us to turn from our old ways of serving our old self (flesh) and the devil, but rather to turn to obey God's will to experience new life in Jesus Christ as our Lord.

"Or **do you not know that the unrighteous will not inherit the kingdom of God?** Do not be deceived: neither the sexually immoral, nor idolaters, nor adulterers, nor men who practice homosexuality, nor thieves, nor the greedy, nor drunkards, nor revilers, nor swindlers will inherit the kingdom of God. And such were some of you. But you were washed, you were sanctified, you were justified in the name of the Lord Jesus Christ and by the Spirit of our God" (1 Corinthians 6:9-11).

"But I say, **walk by the Spirit, and you will not gratify the desires of the flesh**. For the desires of the flesh are against the Spirit, and the desires of the Spirit are against the flesh, for these are opposed to each other, to keep you from doing the things you want to do. But if you are led by the Spirit, you are not under the law. Now the works of the flesh are evident: sexual immorality, impurity, sensuality, idolatry, sorcery, enmity, strife, jealousy, fits of anger, rivalries, dissensions, divisions, envy, drunkenness, orgies, and things like these. I warn you, as I warned you before, that those who do such things **will not inherit the kingdom of God**. But the fruit of the Spirit is love, joy, peace, patience, kindness, goodness, faithfulness, gentleness, self-control; against such things there is no law. **And those who belong to Christ Jesus have crucified the flesh with its passions and desires**" (Galatians 5:16-24).

"For you may be sure of this, that everyone who is sexually immoral or impure, or who is covetous (that is, an idolater), **has no inheritance in the kingdom of Christ and God**. Let no one deceive you with empty words, for because of these things the wrath of God comes upon the sons of disobedience. Therefore, do not become partners with them; for at one time you were darkness, but now you are light in the Lord. **Walk as children of light (for the fruit of light is found in all that is good and right and true), and try to discern what is pleasing to the

Lord. Take no part in the unfruitful works of darkness, but instead expose them" (Ephesians 5:5-11).

"For **the grace of God has appeared, bringing salvation for all people, training us to renounce ungodliness and worldly passions, and to live self-controlled, upright, and godly lives in the present age,** waiting for our blessed hope, the appearing of the glory of our great God and Savior Jesus Christ, who gave himself for us to redeem us from all lawlessness and to purify for himself a people for his own possession who are zealous for good works" (Titus 2:11-14).

"**As obedient children, do not be conformed to the passions of your former ignorance**, but as he who called you is holy, you also **be holy in all your conduct, since it is written, "You shall be holy, for I am holy."** And if you call on him as Father who judges impartially according to each one's deeds, conduct yourselves with fear throughout the time of your exile, knowing that you were ransomed from the futile ways inherited from your forefathers, not with perishable things such as silver or gold, but with the precious blood of Christ, like that of a lamb without blemish or spot" (1 Peter 1:14-19).

In the Kingdom of God, Jesus has defeated the enemy, transferred us from the kingdom of darkness to light, adopted us as His children, and set us apart for a relationship with Him. Our part of the relationship is to know the truth about what God has done for us in Christ Jesus and not succumb to the devil's lies, but to walk in the truth by the power of the Holy Spirit, and to choose to hear God's voice and obey Him. Our obedience to Christ Jesus as our Lord and King blesses us, advances the Kingdom of God, defeats the enemy's kingdom, and brings glory to Jesus.

CHAPTER 10 Questions for Thought and Discussion

1. How does the fact that Jesus defeated Satan and transfer you from the kingdom of darkness to the Kingdom of Light, impact you personally?

2. What lies and doubts of the devil in your life can be defeated by the truth that God "raised us up with him and seat with him in the heavenly places in Christ Jesus" (Ephesians 2:6)

3. What are the truths about 'who you are in Christ' that can defeat the lies of the enemy?

4. How does your obedience to God defeat Satan's work in your life?

5. How does your obedience to Christ expand His Kingdom on this earth?

6. a) What truth do you need to apply to your life?

b) What command do you need to obey?

CHAPTER 11

Relationship with Jesus

"O righteous Father, even though the world does not know you, I know you, and these know that you have sent me. **I made known to them your name**, and I will continue to make it known, **that the love with which you have loved me may be in them, and I in them**" (John 17:25-26).

Here are the last wishes and final words of Jesus found in Jesus's prayer for His followers shortly before His death. They summarize Jesus' purpose in coming to earth and dying on the cross. Jesus came to earth in order to make known His Father's name (meaning who He is), with the purpose that the love of the Father and Jesus' Holy Spirit would be in us. This has been the purpose of God since creation: that His love would be in us—that He would have a place to pour out His love in our hearts—that we would be in a love relationship with Him. The whole reason He sent Jesus to die was so that our relationship with Him would be reconciled. The whole reason He has called and chosen us is to pour His love into our hearts through the Holy Spirit.

"Hope does not put us to shame, because **God's love has been poured into our hearts** through the Holy Spirit who has been given to us" (Romans 5:5).

"In love **he predestined us for adoption as sons through Jesus Christ**, according to the purpose of his will, to the praise of his glorious grace, with which he has blessed us in the Beloved" (Ephesians 1:5-6).

Often in the media, I have heard people mistakenly defining Christianity by what we do. They will say a Christian is someone who keeps the Ten

Commandments, or someone who goes to church, or someone who is good and does kind things. Ever since Jesus died on the cross and reconciled our relationship with God, being a believer is defined in terms of relationship with God, in terms of His great love for us, which He proved in Christ Jesus and our acceptance of His love. Obeying God and doing good things are the fruit of relationship with God, but they are not the goal in themselves. God's desire is for us to love Him and to know Him rather than to do things for Him out of duty or sacrifice. The things we do are an expression of our love for Him.

> "For **I desire steadfast love and not sacrifice**, the knowledge of God rather than burnt offerings" (Hosea 6:6).

> "**Whoever has my commandments and keeps them, he it is who loves me**. And he who loves me will be loved by my Father, and I will love him and manifest myself to him" (John 14:21).

> "I am the vine; you are the branches. **Whoever abides in me and I in him, he it is that bears much fruit,** for apart from me you can do nothing" (John 15:5).

Abiding in God, spending time with Him, getting to know Him, loving Him, and allowing Him to love you will naturally produce good fruit. Being in a relationship with God actually is the only way to produce living fruit, for without God we can do nothing. God never asks us to do for Him what He hasn't already given us and enabled us to do through abiding in Him. Because it is God doing it through us, it will not be difficult or burdensome for us to obey.

> "**For this is the love of God, that we keep his commandments. And his commandments are not burdensome**" (1 John 4:3).

We find that one of the mysteries of God is that with Him there are often antinomies or paradoxes where two beliefs or conclusions that are in themselves reasonable, seem to contradict each other. For example, our love relationship with God bears the good fruit of obedience to God as He is able to work in us. At the same time, our part of loving God in our relationship is by pursuing God through obedience; therefore, we are exhorted often in Scripture to pursue God in various ways. At the same time, we are promised that He has done these very things for us. For example, He exhorts us to pursue godliness but then promises that He has already granted to us all things that pertain to life and godliness.

"Rather **train yourself for godliness**; for while bodily training is of some value, godliness is of value in every way, as it holds promise for the present life and also for the life to come" (1 Timothy 4:7-8).

"**His divine power has granted to us all things that pertain to life and godliness**, through the knowledge of him who called us to his own glory and excellence" (2 Peter 1:3).

We are given the example of Paul, to run the race of life in a disciplined way, but then are reminded that we cannot begin with the Spirit and then depend on the flesh.

"Do you not know that in a race all the runners run, but only one receives the prize? So **run that you may obtain it**. Every athlete exercises self-control in all things. They do it to receive a perishable wreath, but we an imperishable. So, I do not run aimlessly; I do not box as one beating the air. But **I discipline my body and keep it under control**, lest after preaching to others I myself should be disqualified" (1 Corinthians 9:24-27).

"Let me ask you only this: Did you receive the Spirit by works of the law or by hearing with faith? Are you so foolish? **Having begun by the Spirit, are you now being perfected by the flesh**?" (Galatians 3:2-3)

So, we see that there is a paradoxical partnership with God in which we have the responsibility to participate in what He is already doing in our lives. It is not a matter of us taking the initiative to do for Him, rather it is Him initiating in our lives by prompting us to do His will and then giving us the grace and power to do it. Our part is being obedient to get in step with and participate in what God is willing and working in us as a love response to His great love for us.

"Therefore, my beloved, as you have always obeyed, so now... **work out your own salvation with fear and trembling, for it is God who works in you,** both to will and to work for his good pleasure" (Philippians 2:12-13).

Obedience to God is proof that we are in a relationship with God and that we love Him. If we truly love God, we will keep His commandments and it won't be a burden for us to do so. We will delight in pleasing Him and making Him happy. Many times, our relationship with God is compared to a marriage relationship. We do not marry just to have someone to do things for! Being faithful to one partner, earning money to support our family, or cooking and cleaning for our spouse is not the reason and purpose we get married. We get married because we are in love and we want to spend our life with that person. The things we do for that person are not done because of a law that says we have to be faithful, contribute to the marriage, or serve one another. The things we do are because we love that person and want to do things that show our love, and build and protect our relationship.

When we think of what we do in a marriage relationship on earth to respond to love and to build and cultivate that relationship, it is parallel to how we would respond in love to God. How we work out a marriage relationship on earth is similar to how we work out our relationship with God. In a marriage relationship, we want to spend time together, get to know one another, and express our love and admiration for the other. With God, we would want to do the same: spend time with Him, want to get to know who He is, and want to tell Him of our love and adoration of Him. We can spend time with Him, just sitting in His presence meditating on Him and bringing the different facets of our life to Him in prayer. We can get to know Him by reading, studying and hearing the Scriptures, and by listening to His voice. We can love and adore Him by worshiping Him.

Seeking God

Of course, God is always with us wherever we go, for He says He will "never leave us or forsake us" (Hebrews 13:5). "Where shall I go from your Spirit? Or where shall I flee from your presence?" (Psalm 139:7). He is with us at work, play, and school, and He wants to be included in our thoughts regarding all of these things. He is glad to be included in our conversations as well, as we bring the reality of who He is into everyday life. If we again compare Him to a spouse or significant other, like a wife, He enjoys going with us to watch us play a sport, or a video game. Like a husband, He's willing to go with us when we go shopping or out to eat. He wants to be included in our entire life. At the same time, like in every love relationship, He wants to have His own special time with us where He has our undivided attention, where we look on Him face to face, and where we leave our world to seek Him in the Spirit. Like every intimate relationship, He wants time when we put all other activities, thoughts, and worries aside and seek Him.

The best way to do this is waiting on Him in meditation and prayer. Waiting on Him is a time when we invite Him to meet with us and we sit in His presence. Sometimes we can feel His presence, sometimes we don't, but by faith we sit, knowing that He has heard our prayer and has promised to be with us. In His presence, whether we feel Him or not, His Spirit is there connecting us to God, giving us life and strength in our inner being, filling us with His love, filling us with the fullness of God. In His presence, we will find life and fullness of joy that satisfies our soul.

> "That according to the riches of his glory he may grant you to be strengthened with power through his Spirit in your inner being, so that **Christ may dwell in your hearts through faith**—that you, being rooted and grounded in love, may have strength to comprehend with all the saints what is the breadth and length and height and depth, and **to know the love of Christ that surpasses knowledge, that you may be filled with all the fullness of God**" (Ephesians 3:16-19).

> "You make known to me the path of life; **in your presence there is fullness of joy**; at your right hand are pleasures forevermore" (Psalm 16:11).

As we sit in His presence, we can focus on Jesus, meditating on who He is, and calling on His name. We can meditate on words from Scripture or all that Jesus did for us on the cross; remember the great things and miracles He has done for us; thank and praise Him for His wondrous works; seek Him for His strength, seek more of His presence.

> "Oh, give thanks to the LORD; call upon his name; make known his deeds among the peoples! Sing to him, sing praises to him; tell of all his wondrous works! Glory in his holy name; let the hearts of those who seek the LORD rejoice! **Seek the LORD and his strength; seek his presence continually**! Remember the wondrous works that he has done, his miracles, and the judgments he uttered" (Psalm 105:1-5).

In His presence is the place of prayer where we can pour out our hearts to God, inviting Him into every part of our lives, giving Him every concern, worry, hurt, pain; asking Him to work and transform every problem; entrusting to Him everyone and everything we are responsible for; surrendering every facet of our lives in dependence on Him. What relief to bring our lives to Him and not have to carry it by ourselves!

> "**Come to me**, all who labor and are heavy laden, and I will give you rest. **Take my yoke upon you, and learn from me**, for I am gentle and

lowly in heart, and you will find rest for your souls. For my yoke is easy, and my burden is light" (Matthew 11:28-30).

"**Do not be anxious about anything**, but in everything by prayer and supplication with thanksgiving **let your requests be made known to God**. And the peace of God, which surpasses all understanding, will guard your hearts and your minds in Christ Jesus" (Philippians 4:6-7).

God's Holy Spirit speaks to us by highlighting the Scriptures to our hearts, and in prayer we hear His still small voice respond to the cries of our hearts. As we said in Chapter 1, there is no limit to the ways God is constantly speaking to us. Prayer is our opportunity to quiet our hearts and minds in God's presence to wait on Him, to listen for a word He may speak to our hearts or minds to satisfy our souls, and to mediate on the Scriptures.

"And **your ears shall hear a word** behind you, saying, "This is the way, walk in it," when you turn to the right or when you turn to the left" (Isaiah 30:21).

"Come, everyone who thirsts, come to the waters; and he who has no money, come, buy and eat! Come, buy wine and milk without money and without price. Why do you spend your money for that which is not bread, and your labor for that which does not satisfy? Listen diligently to me, and eat what is good, and delight yourselves in rich food. **Incline your ear, and come to me; hear, that your soul may live**" (Isaiah 55:1-3).

"Thus says the LORD who made the earth, the LORD who formed it to establish it—the LORD is his name: **Call to me and I will answer you, and will tell you great and hidden things that you have not known**" (Jeremiah 33:3).

"Now we have received not the spirit of the world, but the Spirit who is from God, that we might understand the things freely given us by God. And we impart this in words not taught by human wisdom but **taught by the Spirit, interpreting spiritual truths to those who are spiritual**" (1 Corinthians 2:12-13).

"That the God of our Lord Jesus Christ, the Father of glory, may give you **the Spirit of wisdom and of revelation in the knowledge of him**, having the eyes of your hearts enlightened, that you may know what is the hope to which he has called you" (Ephesians 1:17-18).

"Therefore, as the Holy Spirit says, "Today, **if you hear his voice**, do not harden your hearts as in the rebellion, on the day of testing in the wilderness" (Hebrews 3:7-8).

Knowing God

"**Let us know; let us press on to know the LORD**; his going out is sure as the dawn; he will come to us as the showers, as the spring rains that water the earth" (Hosea 6:3).

I love this verse! I still remember the first time I read that verse and how it stirred my heart with passion to know the Lord; to purpose to know Him as well as I possibly could. I was and still am moved to tears at the promise that He surely will come to us, He will reveal Himself to us. He is as predictable as the dawn comes in the morning; as refreshing and life-giving as the spring rains. There is only one thing worth seeking, one thing worth giving our lives to, and that is to know the Lord.

"One thing have I asked of the LORD, that will I seek after: that I may dwell in the house of the LORD all the days of my life, to gaze upon the beauty of the LORD and to inquire in his temple" (Psalm 27:4).

He is worth knowing because He is beautiful! He is delightful! In this verse "the beauty of the Lord" can be translated "the delightfulness of the Lord." Oh, to gaze upon Him, to inquire of Him, to listen to His voice, to know Him better. Nothing can satisfy our soul more than knowing God Himself!

"O God, you are my God; **earnestly I seek you; my soul thirsts for you; my flesh faints for you**, as in a dry and weary land where there is no water. **So, I have looked upon you in the sanctuary, beholding your power and glory**. Because your steadfast love is better than life, **my lips will praise you. So, I will bless you as long as I live; in your name I will lift up my hands. My soul will be satisfied** as with fat and rich food, and my mouth will praise you with joyful lips, when **I remember you upon my bed**, and **meditate on you in the watches of the night**; for you have been my help, and in the shadow of your wings I will sing for joy. **My soul clings to you**; your right hand upholds me" (Psalm 63:1-8).

If a husband and wife were temporarily separated, they would phone, text, Skype, write letters, or correspond by email. Those letters would be read over and over again as the couple waited to be reunited. We too have been given a letter from God, telling us all about who He is, what He has done in the past, His dreams for us, and His plans for the future. As we grow in love with Him, we will hang on to His every word, and organize our lives around what He has written that pertains to us. We will cherish every word that helps us to know Him better. The letter God has given us has been preserved for us in the Bible. The best way to get to know God is to study and meditate on this written word of God. Moses, to whom God gave the first five books of the Bible to write, warned the Israelites that the words of God were the difference between life and death, between blessing and curse. He exhorted them to choose life that they might live. Later he reminded them that these words of God were not idle or empty words for them, but that they were life itself!

> "I call heaven and earth to witness against you today, that I have set before you life and death, blessing and curse. **Therefore, choose life** that you and your offspring may live, loving the LORD your God, **obeying his voice and holding fast to him, for he is your life** and length of days" (Deuteronomy 30:19-20).

> "Take to heart all the words by which I am warning you today, that you may command them to your children, that they may **be careful to do all the words of this law. For it is no empty word for you, but your very life, and by this word you shall live long** in the land that you are going over the Jordan to possess" (Deuteronomy 32:46-47).

We are exhorted to be like a workman able to "rightly handle the word of truth" and to "pay attention to words of Scripture as a lamp shining in a dark place." The words of the Bible proclaim that they are "able to make us wise unto salvation, are profitable for teaching, reproof, correction and training in righteousness," and are able to "equip us for every good work."

> "Do your best to present yourself to God as one approved, a worker who has no need to be ashamed, **rightly handling the word of truth**" (2 Timothy 2:15).

> "The sacred writings, which are **able to make you wise for salvation** through faith in Christ Jesus. All Scripture is breathed out by God and

profitable for teaching, for reproof, for correction, and for training in righteousness, that the man of God may be complete, equipped for every good work" (2 Timothy 3:15-17).

"And **we have the prophetic word more fully confirmed**, to which you will do well to pay attention as to a lamp shining in a dark place, until the day dawns and the morning star rises in your hearts, knowing this first of all, that no prophecy of Scripture comes from someone's own interpretation. For no prophecy was ever produced by the will of man, but **men spoke from God as they were carried along by the Holy Spirit**" (2 Peter 1:19-21).

The context of 2 Peter 1 tells us that the written word of God is more reliable than if we audibly heard the voice of God from heaven (see 2 Peter 1:16-19). In Galatians 1:8, Paul says that the good news about Jesus that he proclaimed is more trustworthy than if an angel appeared from heaven to give us a new message. According to the above verses, we find that all Scripture is the very word of God: "breathed out by God" and that "men spoke from God as they were carried along by the Holy Spirit." Because they are the very words of God, they are powerful to change our life at the very core of our being. The word of God can go where we cannot in the flesh; it can pierce to the division of soul and spirit, and can discern the thoughts and intentions of the heart.

"For **the word of God is living and active, sharper than any two-edged sword, piercing to the division of soul and of spirit**, of joints and of marrow, and **discerning the thoughts and intentions of the heart**" (Hebrews 4:12).

If you 'eat' the written word of God, it has power to give life to your soul and be your source of great joy. Eating Scripture means to delight in and mediate on the word of God. If you delight in and meditate on the word of the Lord, you will be blessed, fruitful, and prosper. Eating, delighting in, and meditating on the word of God are the prerequisites to receiving these blessings.

"The law of the LORD is perfect, reviving the soul; the testimony of the LORD is sure, making wise the simple; the precepts of the LORD are right, rejoicing the heart; the commandment of the LORD is pure, enlightening the eyes; the fear of the LORD is clean, enduring forever; the rules of the LORD are true, and righteous altogether. More to be

> desired are they than gold, even much fine gold; sweeter also than honey and drippings of the honeycomb" (Psalm 19:7-10).

> "How sweet are your words to my taste, sweeter than honey to my mouth!" (Psalm 119:103).

> "Your words were found, **and I ate them**, and your words became to me a joy and the delight of my heart, for I am called by your name, O LORD, God of hosts" (Jeremiah 16:15).

> "Blessed is the man who walks not in the counsel of the wicked, nor stands in the way of sinners, nor sits in the seat of scoffers; but **his delight is in the law of the LORD, and on his law he meditates day and night**. He is like a tree planted by streams of water that yields its fruit in its season, and its leaf does not wither. In all that he does, he prospers" (Psalm 1:1-3).

Loving God

> "Hear, O Israel: The LORD our God, the LORD is one. **You shall love the LORD your God with all your heart and with all your soul and with all your might**" (Deuteronomy 6:4-5).

> "And **you shall love the Lord your God with all your heart and with all your soul and with all your mind and with all your strength**" (Mark 12:30).

From the beginning of the Old Testament until now, God has desired our love. Loving God is the summary of all the law and commandments in the Bible. If we love God as our first priority, all other things will fall into place. Loving God is the most important commandment. The above verse was the answer Jesus gave to the question, "Which commandment is the most important of all?" Jesus answered, "The most important is, 'Hear, O Israel: The Lord our God, the Lord is one. And you shall love the Lord your God with all your heart and with all your soul and with all your mind and with all your strength" (Mark 12:28-30).

The question now is how can we love God? We have already talked about how we can prove our love by obeying the word of God. Besides our actions, in a marriage relationship we long to hear our spouse tell us they love us, expound on all the things they like about us, and express their undying commitment to us. We would be glad to hear these words every day. God is the same way. He enjoys hearing our expressions of love and adoration. He created us so that we would glorify Him.

> "Everyone who is called by my name, whom I created for my glory, whom I formed and made" (Isaiah 43:7).

> "Ascribe to the LORD the glory due his name; worship the LORD in the splendor of holiness" (Psalm 29:2).

> "Oh come, let us worship and bow down; let us kneel before the LORD, our Maker!" (Psalm 95:6).

> "Worship the LORD in the splendor of holiness; tremble before him, all the earth!" (Psalm 96:9)

I have come to realize that the very best and most meaningful thing that I can give God is my praise and worship. More than serving Him, more than loving and helping other people on the earth, more than all the religious things that might be done, simple words of praise, adoration, and love are the very best we can give God. Our worship is the one thing we have to offer Him that He hasn't already done for us, and even in that we must depend on His Holy Spirit to empower our worship for "God is spirit, and those who worship him must worship in spirit and truth" (John 4:24). Even our worship comes from God and is an awesome privilege to participate with the Holy Spirit in.

> "Blessed are you, O LORD, the God of Israel our father, forever and ever. Yours, O LORD, is the greatness and the power and the glory and the victory and the majesty, for all that is in the heavens and in the earth is yours. Yours is the kingdom, O LORD, and you are exalted as head above all. Both riches and honor come from you, and you rule over all. In your hand are power and might, and in your hand it is to make great and to give strength to all. And now we thank you, our God, and praise your glorious name. But who am I, and what is my people, that we should be able thus to offer willingly? For all things come from you, and of your own have we given you" (1 Chronicles 29:10-14).

This passage, as well as many of the Psalms, was written by King David. In the Book of Psalms, we are led over and over again into songs of worship. Later in

Scripture, it says that David was "a man after God's own heart" (1 Samuel 13:14; Acts 13:22). From the Psalms, we get a view into David's heart, which was continually full of worship, thanks, praise, and adoration. Reading and praying the Psalms are a great place to start in a life of worship. Throughout history, there have been great hymns written in worship of God, and today there is awesome worship written to modern music that focuses on Jesus and lifts up and exalts His name. The best way I know to worship and express my love to God is to join my heart and voice to sing worship songs directed to Jesus.

> "Oh come, let us sing to the LORD; let us make a joyful noise to the rock of our salvation! Let us come into his presence with thanksgiving; let us make a joyful noise to him with songs of praise!" (Psalm 95:1-2)

> "Make a joyful noise to the LORD, all the earth! Serve the LORD with gladness! Come into his presence with singing! Know that the LORD, he is God! It is he who made us, and we are his; we are his people, and the sheep of his pasture. Enter his gates with thanksgiving, and his courts with praise! Give thanks to him; bless his name! For the LORD is good; his steadfast love endures forever, and his faithfulness to all generations" (Psalm 100:1-5).

> "I will extol you, my God and King, and bless your name forever and ever. Every day I will bless you and praise your name forever and ever. Great is the LORD, and greatly to be praised, and his greatness is unsearchable. One generation shall commend your works to another, and shall declare your mighty acts. On the glorious splendor of your majesty, and on your wondrous works, I will meditate. They shall speak of the might of your awesome deeds, and I will declare your greatness. They shall pour forth the fame of your abundant goodness and shall sing aloud of your righteousness. The LORD is gracious and merciful; slow to anger and abounding in steadfast love. The LORD is good to all, and his mercy is over all that he has made. All your works shall give thanks to you, O LORD, and all your saints shall bless you! They shall speak of the glory of your kingdom and tell of your power, to make known to the children of man your mighty deeds, and the glorious splendor of your kingdom. Your kingdom is an everlasting kingdom, and your dominion endures throughout all generations" (Psalm 145:1-13).

A Few More Basics

"Now when they heard this they were cut to the heart, and said to Peter and the rest of the apostles, "Brothers, what shall we do?" And Peter said to them, "Repent and **be baptized** every one of you in the name of Jesus Christ for the forgiveness of your sins, and you will receive the gift of the Holy Spirit. For the promise is for you and for your children and for all who are far off, everyone whom the Lord our God calls to himself." And with many other words he bore witness and continued to exhort them, saying, "Save yourselves from this crooked generation." So **those who received his word were baptized**, and there were added that day about three thousand souls. And they devoted themselves to the **apostles' teaching** and the **fellowship**, to the **breaking of bread** and the **prayers**. And all who believed were together and **had all things in common**. And they were selling their possessions and belongings and **distributing the proceeds to all, as any had need**. And day by day, **attending the temple together and breaking bread in their homes**, they received their food with glad and generous hearts, praising God and having favor with all the people. And the Lord added to their number day by day those who were being saved" (Acts 2:37-47).

Let us look one more time at the passage in Acts 2 at Pentecost when the baptism of the Holy Spirit came, and 3,000 people came to believe that Jesus was the Christ and made Him their Savior and Lord. What did the new believers do after they were saved that we can pattern our lives as believers after? This passage says that they were baptized, devoted themselves to teaching of the word, prayer, fellowship, breaking of bread, attending the temple, and sharing everything they had with each other. We have already talked about the word and prayer, which leaves us giving, baptism, fellowship, and breaking of bread.

Giving

"Now the full number of those who believed were of one heart and soul, and **no one said that any of the things that belonged to him was his own, but they had everything in common...There was not a needy person among them**, for as many as were owners of lands or houses sold them and brought the proceeds of what was sold and laid it at the apostles' feet, and it was distributed to each as any had need" (Acts 4:32,34,35).

In recent days "having all things in common" and "selling their possessions and belongings and distributing the proceeds to all, as any had need" has been practiced by "church giving" or and "charitable donations." This clearly has not risen to the sacrifice that was made in the above passage. However, this may be something God does again in the future, especially in the end times when the need will be great. In the meantime, we will be blessed if, as an act of worship and thanksgiving to God, we give to Him by supporting the church, mission work, and benevolence to those less fortunate. By giving something back to God we are acknowledging that all things come from God, therefore, belong to God; and in gratitude for all He has given us, we give back to him.

> "'Bring the whole tithe into the storehouse, so that there may be food in My house, and test Me now in this,' says the LORD of hosts, 'if I will not open for you the windows of heaven and pour out for you a blessing until it overflows'" (Malachi 3:10).

Baptism

> "There is one body and one Spirit—just as you were called to the one hope that belongs to your call one Lord, one faith, **one baptism**, one God and Father of all, who is over all and through all and in all" (Ephesians 4:4-6).

> "Repent and **be baptized every one of you** in the name of Jesus Christ for the forgiveness of your sins" (Acts 2:37)

Peter's response to the people when they asked what they should do was to "repent and be baptized". We have talked about repenting in Chapter 6. Immediately upon repentance and receiving Jesus as Savior and Lord is the time to be baptized. According to Jesus' final instruction to the disciples before ascending to heaven, baptism was the first step after becoming His follower. "Go therefore and make disciples of all nations, baptizing them in the name of the Father and of the Son and of the Holy Spirit" (Matthew 28:19). Water baptism signifies identifying with Jesus' death on the cross and resurrection. It is also a public statement that we have chosen to deny our old self, take up the cross and follow Christ. Our participating in the act of being baptized is a step of faith to receive the powerful working of God to give us new resurrection life. In parts of the world, baptism is the time we make a public change of our religion and is a step that is taken very seriously because it may cost the individual their family, job, community, or even their life.

> "We were buried therefore with him by baptism into death, in order that, just as Christ was raised from the dead by the glory of the Father, we too might walk in newness of life" (Romans 6:4).

> "Having been buried with him in baptism, in which you were also raised with him through faith in the powerful working of God, who raised him from the dead" (Colossians 2:12).

Where baptism in the physical is symbolic, in the Spirit, it is reality. Baptism confirms in the Spirit that the old is being done away with and new life being born. From my over 20 years of experience in inner-healing ministry, I believe that the time of baptism is a really good time to take a thorough inventory of our old lifestyle, renounce sin out loud, and ask for deliverance, healing, and new life for the following four major areas of our old life:

1) **Idolatry** by yourself or your ancestors through participating in other religions (i.e. Islam, Buddhism, Hinduism, Mormonism, Native American worship, etc.), and cults (occult, witchcraft, Wicca, Free Masonry, New Age, etc.)
2) **Unforgiveness** and bitterness toward anyone who has sinned against you
3) **Sexual activity** outside of marriage between a man and a woman
4) **Addictions** such as drugs, alcohol, pornography, sex, etc.

In the early church and currently in some traditional denominations, at water baptism a person renounces "all the devil's works and ways" in their life. With the increase in the above activities, which Satan is using in believer's lives to deceive them and keep them in bondage to their old self, renouncing these things and asking for deliverance and healing at baptism, at the start of your relationship with Jesus, may prevent a lot of pain, suffering, and defeat.

Fellowship, Breaking of Bread, Breaking Bread in Their Homes

As soon as possible after making a decision for Christ, Scripture encourages us to be baptized; however, this usually requires a relationship with other believers who can do the baptizing. Baptism and the breaking of bread, otherwise called Lord's Supper, are two things that usually take place in a church setting. Although it is possible to have good fellowship outside of a church, there is a need to be part of a church fellowship in order to be baptized and to participate regularly in the Lord's Supper. Jesus celebrated the Lord's Supper with His followers the day before His death. At that time, Jesus said to do this in remembrance of Him because "as often as you eat this bread and drink the cup, you proclaim the Lord's death until he comes." There are so many things to be remembered in the wine and the bread which proclaim the blood and body of Christ and all that was accomplished in Jesus' death. These things are good for us to bring to mind over and over again. What is symbolic physically in the Lord's Supper has spiritual reality and power in the Spirit that impacts our lives; therefore, you will be blessed if you partake of the Lord's Supper on a regular basis.

> "Now as they were eating, Jesus took bread, and after blessing it broke it and gave it to the disciples, and said, 'Take, eat; this is my body.' And he took a cup, and when he had given thanks, he gave it to them, saying, 'Drink of it, all of you, for this is my blood of the covenant, which is poured out for many for the forgiveness of sins. I tell you I will not drink again of this fruit of the vine until that day when I drink it new with you in my Father's kingdom'" (Matthew 26:26-29).

> "For I received from the Lord what I also delivered to you, that the Lord Jesus on the night when he was betrayed took bread, and when he had given thanks, he broke it, and said, 'This is my body which is for you. Do this in remembrance of me.' In the same way also he took the cup, after supper, saying, 'This cup is the new covenant in my blood. Do this, as often as you drink it, in remembrance of me.' For as often as you eat this bread and drink the cup, you proclaim the Lord's death until he comes" (1 Corinthians 11:23-26).

The definition of fellowship is a group of people who share companionship, friendship, mutual experiences, activities, and interests. Acts 2 tells us that the new believers attended the temple together day by day. It was there they could fellowship with other believers by hearing the apostles teaching the word of God, and being encouraged in their faith by other believers. We are exhorted in Scripture to meet together regularly as believers, to encourage one another and be encouraged by other believers. Although God meets with each of us individually, when we as a group invite Jesus, there is a special blessing of His presence as He promises to be where two or three are gathered together in His name.

> "And let us consider how to stir up one another to love and good works, not neglecting to meet together, as is the habit of some, but encouraging one another, and all the more as you see the Day drawing near" (Hebrews 10:24-25).

> "For where two or three are gathered in my name, there am I among them" (Matthew 18:20).

There are some blessings and answers to prayer that God limits Himself to doing through His body, the church. Each of us is a part of the body of Christ. To have all our needs met, we need to connect with the other parts of His body. We have something to offer that other people need, and they have things to bless us. With all the parts of the body working together, God can flow through us all to meet all the needs individuals might have. Without all believers, some needs go unmet. Be encouraged that you are a special part of Christ's body and you will be a great blessing to other people if you make yourself available. You will also be blessed by other believers' ministry to you. This is true in fellowship wherever we meet with two or three believers, inside or out of the church.

> "For just as the body is one and has many members, and all the members of the body, though many, are one body, so it is with Christ. For the body does not consist of one member but of many. But as it is, God arranged the members in the body, each one of them, as he chose. If all were a single member, where would the body be? As it is, there are many parts, yet one body. If one member suffers, all suffer together; if one member is honored, all rejoice together" (1 Corinthians 12: 12, 14, 18, 19, 20, 26).

The new believers were said to be "breaking bread in their homes" or "from house to house" (see Acts 2:46) which sounds like having people over for dinner; fellowshipping around the dinner table; getting to know one another in the home setting where you really can get to know who people are. Then too, throughout the years and around the world, many moves of God have involved "home groups" or "house churches" where more than two or three people get together to worship, pray, study the Bible, and minister to one another in their homes. Two good descriptions of biblical home groups might be:

> "When you come together, each one has a hymn, a lesson, a revelation, a tongue, or an interpretation. Let all things be done for building up" (1 Corinthians 14:26).

"Addressing one another in psalms and hymns and spiritual songs, singing and making melody to the Lord with your heart, giving thanks always and for everything to God the Father in the name of our Lord Jesus Christ" (Ephesians 5:19-20).

As a new believer, it would be great if you could find a church and a home group where you can fellowship with other believers who could help you grow in your faith. Discerning which is a good church or home group to attend has the same considerations as testing for evidence of the Holy Spirit. Do they focus on Jesus and getting to know Jesus better, spend time studying the Bible to get the mind of Christ, have godly Spirit-filled character and fruit, and demonstrate love above all else? Of course, churches and home groups are made of humans so no church will be perfect, but these are the basic conditions for a good fellowship.

Mystery of Relationship with Jesus

The greatest mystery about a relationship with God is that He is the one who wanted a relationship with us and initiated it. He is the one who sent Jesus Christ to die on the cross to restore the possibility of relationship with Him. He is the one who sent His Holy Spirit into our hearts so that He could dwell with us and abide with us. He is the one who first chose us; we responded to His call and choosing. He is the one who designed us and knows us perfectly and still loved us first, just as we were. He is the one who gives us the grace to pursue Him, to seek Him, to get to know Him, to love Him.

"**You did not choose me, but I chose you** and appointed you that you should go and bear fruit and that your fruit should abide" (John 15:16).

"In this is love, not that we have loved God but that he loved us and sent his Son to be the propitiation for our sins. **We love because he first loved us**" (1 John 3:10, 19).

Seeking, knowing, and loving God, along with the basics of giving, baptism, the Lord's Supper, and fellowship are a few of the things that build a relationship with God. Keeping your eyes on Jesus, focusing on Him, spending time with Him, making Him the priority of your thoughts, time, energy, and resources will allow you to know Him better and love Him more. The more you know Him, the more you will love and worship Him. The more you love Him, then the more you seek Him and want more of His presence and to know Him better. This cycle continues all through your life as a believer for we can never exhaust the mystery of God in Christ Jesus. There will always be more to know, more to fall in love with, more to praise. We will spend all of eternity in heaven discovering the mystery of Jesus Christ and enjoying being in His presence and getting to know Him.

CHAPTER 11 Questions for Thought and Discussion

1. What are the key elements of having a relationship with God?

2. Who is responsible for developing a relationship with God—what is our responsibility, what is God's responsibility?

3. Why is mediating on the Scriptures so important for your relationship with God?

4. How can we develop our love for God with our heart, with our soul, with our mind, and with our strength?

   "The most important is, 'Hear, O Israel: The Lord our God, the Lord is one. And you shall love the Lord your God with all your heart and with all your soul and with all your mind and with all your strength.'" Mark 12:30

5. a) What resistance or fears do you have when considering looking for a church or home fellowship?

   b) How can you process those hindrances so that you are free to enter into fellowship with other believers?

6. What specific changes to your schedule will you need to make to include time with Jesus?

CHAPTER 12

Grace and Glory

"For the LORD God is a sun and shield; **the LORD will give grace and glory**; no good thing will He withhold from them that walk uprightly" (Psalm 84:11).

"And the Word became flesh and dwelt among us, and we have seen his **glory, glory** as of the only Son from the Father, full of **grace** and truth... For from his fullness we have all received, **grace upon grace**. For the law was given through Moses; **grace** and truth came through Jesus Christ. No one has ever seen God; the only God, who is at the Father's side, he has made him known" (John 1:14-18).

"**He is the radiance of the glory of God** and the exact imprint of his nature, and he upholds the universe by the word of his power" (Hebrews 1:3).

Glory is defined as the self-manifestation of who God is in any way He chooses to reveal Himself. The greatest way God has chosen to reveal Himself is in the person of Christ Jesus. God, who dwells in unapproachable light and cannot be seen by man, has revealed Himself in Jesus, who in the visible form of man, come to make the Father known. Jesus became flesh and dwelt among us making the Father known, revealing the glory of God. Jesus is "the radiance of the glory of God and the exact imprint of his nature" (Hebrews 1:3). Jesus Himself is the manifestation of the revelation of God the Father. Therefore, Jesus is the glory! There is nothing that Jesus can do, give, or manifest that is more glorious than Himself. Therefore, it is only Jesus we must seek when we want to experience the glory of God. God has been so gracious to us of late to manifest Himself in so many ways—making His presence known in times of worshiping Him, healing the sick, revealing Himself in dreams and visions, and all the other ways He makes Himself known to draw people's hearts to Himself. All of these manifestations of Jesus have their source in who Jesus is. Therefore, Jesus Himself is the only One we must seek because He is the glory in all manifestations. If we seek the manifestation instead of Jesus, we are missing the glory—the glory is in Jesus, glory of the only Son from the Father.

> "The mystery hidden for ages and generations but now revealed to his saints. To them God chose to make known how great among the Gentiles are the riches of the glory of this mystery, which is **Christ in you, the hope of glory**" (Colossians 1:26-27).

According to Colossians 1 "Christ in you" is our "hope of glory." Because of His gracious favor on us since we invited Jesus into our lives, Jesus dwells within our hearts, manifesting the glory of God in us. Christ in us is our only hope of glory! He is our glory! Our glory can only be found in "Christ in us," "Christ shining His light in our hearts," and "Christ dwelling in our hearts." It is clear that the glory is not ours; He is the treasure that is in us. The glory is Jesus' glory overshadowing us, filling our hearts with Himself, conforming us to the image of His glory one degree at a time by the power of His Spirit in us. What underserved favor!!!

> "For God, who said, 'Let light shine out of darkness,' has **shone in our hearts** to give the light of the knowledge of **the glory of God** in the face of Jesus Christ" (2 Corinthians 4:6).

> "That according to **the riches of his glory** he may grant you to be strengthened with power through his Spirit in your inner being, so that **Christ may dwell in your hearts** through faith" (Ephesians 3:16).

> "And we all, with unveiled face, **beholding the glory of the Lord, are being transformed into the same image from one degree of glory to another**. For this comes from the Lord who is the Spirit" (2 Corinthians 3:18).

Jesus is the glory and the grace of God. According to John 1, the glory of God is manifested in the amazing grace that Jesus lavishly pours out on us. In Christ Jesus we have received "grace upon grace" (John 1:16). Grace is simply defined as "God's favor" which encompasses every aspect of the Christian life from the time He has drawn us out of the miry clay pit of destruction (see Psalm 40:2) until the day He comes to bring us to Himself for an eternity of glory. It is all grace. Grace is God's loving-kindness and goodness to do for us that which we cannot do for ourselves that is completely unearned or deserved on our part. Grace is God revealing in us the glory that is found in Jesus Christ. In this chapter, we will look at four aspects of God's grace which reveal His glory: 1) to rescue, forgive, and save us from our sin and our sinful state of destruction; 2) to purify and sanctify us to make us holy; 3) to empower us for our calling to do good works which He has prepared beforehand that we should walk in; 4) to empower us to participate in the things that Jesus is doing by the power of the Holy Spirit.

It is in the grace that we have in Jesus Christ, Him living in us, that we can do anything for "in him we live and move and have our being" (Acts 17:28); and "from him and through him and to him are all things. To him be glory forever. Amen" (Romans 11:36). He is our source of glory. It is His amazing loving and kind favor on us that makes everything possible, for without Him we can do nothing (see John 15:5). We are exhorted to continue to grow and be strong in the grace that is found in the Lord Jesus. How can we grow and be strong in grace if it is totally an unmerited gift of God's loving-kindness? The only way I know is to use the grace that is given us, and to ask for more. We are warned not "to receive the grace of God in vain" (2 Corinthians 6:1); to "nullify the grace of God" (Galatians 2:21); to "fall from grace" (Galatians 5:4). We miss God's grace by depending on our self and going our own way. We grow strong in God's grace when we depend on God and receive His favor and strength to go His way instead of our own.

"**Be strong in the grace** that is in Christ Jesus" (2 Timothy 2:1).

"But **grow in the grace** and knowledge of our Lord and Savior Jesus Christ. To him be the glory both now and to the day of eternity. Amen" (1 Peter 3:18).

Grace and Glory of Salvation

"But God, being rich in mercy, because of the great love with which he loved us, even when we were dead in our trespasses, made us alive together with Christ—**by grace you have been saved**— and raised us up with him and seated us with him in the heavenly places in Christ Jesus, so that in the coming ages he might show the immeasurable riches of his **grace** in kindness toward us in Christ Jesus. For **by grace you have been saved through faith.** And this is not your own doing; it is the gift of God, not a result of works, so that no one may boast" (Ephesians 2:4-9).

God not only revealed Himself to us in Jesus Christ, but because of His love for us while we were dead in our sin, Christ died for us. This is the grace of God. In grace, God looked on us in our lowly, helpless, sinful state with compassion and pity. When we were deserving of punishment and destruction, He gave us favor because of His infinite goodness and loving-kindness without considering our own effort or works. Now we have obtained access into this grace, the amazing favor of God in which we stand, and we rejoice in hope of the glory of God, the revelation of Himself to us.

> "Therefore, since we have been justified by faith, we have peace with God through our Lord Jesus Christ. Through him **we have also obtained access by faith into this grace in which we stand,** and **we rejoice in hope of the glory of God**" (Romans 5:2).

According to this verse "we have obtained access into this grace in which we stand." Grace is a position we have "in Christ Jesus." Everything we talked about in Chapter 8 that is ours "in Christ Jesus" is because of the favor or grace of God. Grace is an eternal position in Christ, which we have been placed before God since the minute we invited Christ into our lives as Savior and Lord. Our position in Christ is completely secure. We are forgiven, made righteous, and reconciled to God based on the work of the cross not based on anything we have done or not done. Therefore, it is impossible to add to or take away from our position in Christ Jesus. Our position is in Christ and is not dependent on what we do but on what Christ Jesus did on the cross. In Christ, the work is finished and we are complete. We stand before God and He only sees the righteous holiness of our Lord Jesus. The awesome thing about grace is, God has done it all—Jesus Christ has done everything we need for salvation in His death and resurrection.

> "I will greatly rejoice in the LORD; my soul shall exult in my God, for he has clothed me with the garments of salvation; he has covered me with the robe of righteousness, as a bridegroom decks himself like a priest with a beautiful headdress, and as a bride adorns herself with her jewels" (Isaiah 61:10).

The good news continues; grace does not stop with salvation! Not only are we saved by grace as a gift of God not requiring works, but it is also the free favor of God that transforms our lives to be holy. It is the grace of God that will enable us to do the good works which God has pre-planned for us, and it is the grace of God which empowers us with the Holy Spirit to do those things which only God can do. Grace did not just save us; it enables us to live the saved life! It is the grace of God that transforms our life!

Cheap or Costly Grace

"Knowing that you were ransomed from the futile ways inherited from your forefathers, **not with perishable things such as silver or gold, but with the precious blood of Christ,** like that of a lamb without blemish or spot" (1 Peter 1:18-19).

"For the love of Christ controls us, because we have concluded this: that one has died for all, therefore all have died; and he died for all, **that those who live might no longer live for themselves but for him** who for their sake died and was raised" (2 Corinthians 5:14-15).

The grace of God, that is freely given and completely unearned or merited, cost Jesus His life. We were not ransomed with gold or silver but with the blood of Christ Jesus. Because He gave His life for us, the cost of following Him is for us to give our lives to Him. Even though the gift is free, the response to grace is costly and requires complete surrender of our lives to follow Jesus. This will cost us everything. This requires dying to ourselves and allowing Him to live His life in us.

The idea of "cheap grace" in contrast to "costly grace" comes from a famous book called *The Cost of Discipleship* by Dietrich Bonhoeffer who was a pastor who gave up his life to stay true to Jesus during the time of the Nazi regime in Germany. "Cheap grace" expects the free gift of God's grace to come without a response from the receiver. I believe a theology of cheap grace comes from misunderstanding the difference between "positional grace" which provides our position in Christ, and the "present grace" in which we participate walking out our salvation in everyday life. Our positional grace in Christ is the grace of our salvation which remains unchanged, eternal, and secure before God regardless of what we do because it is based on Jesus' righteousness and holiness, not our own. However, we also have the responsibility to live our life walking in the present grace and power of the Holy Spirit to grow spiritually, fulfill our calling, and do the works that Jesus is doing in and through us. Jesus is always working in us to cause us to will and to work for His good pleasure.

"Therefore, my beloved, as you have always obeyed, so now, not only as in my presence but much more in my absence, **work out your own salvation with fear and trembling, for it is God who works in you, both to will and to work for his good pleasure**" (Philippians 2:12-13).

Grace and Glory of Sanctification

> "And now I commend you to God and to the word of **his grace**, which is able to build you up and to give you the inheritance among all those who are **sanctified**" (Acts 20:32).

> "For the **grace of God** has appeared, bringing salvation for all people, **training us** to renounce ungodliness and worldly passions, and to live self-controlled, upright, and godly lives in the present age" (Titus 2:11-12).

> "The **God of all grace**, who has called you to his eternal glory in Christ, **will himself restore, confirm, strengthen, and establish you**" (1 Peter 5:10).

According to the above verses, after we are saved, the grace of God sanctifies us, which means to begin the process of purifying us and making us holy by separating us from sin, consecrating us unto God. It is the process whereby our righteous holy position in Christ Jesus gains increasing access into our present life on this earth. It is the release of the Holy Spirit, who filled our spirits when we invited Jesus into our lives, to expand into our souls and bodies which transforms of our will, thoughts, emotions, and consequent actions. It is God's goal that our spirit, soul and body are sanctified.

> "Now may the God of peace himself **sanctify you completely, and may your whole spirit and soul and body be kept blameless** at the coming of our Lord Jesus Christ. He who calls you is faithful; he will surely do it" (1 Thessalonians 5:23-24).

The above verses promise that it is the grace of God that transforms us. In them God promises us His grace to: build us up and give us the inheritance; train us to renounce ungodliness and worldly passions; train us to live self-controlled, upright and godly lives; and to restore, confirm, strengthen, and establish us. A whole book could be written on each of these works of grace in our lives as we allow Jesus to live His life through us. It is by His grace that He manifests His life in us in these various ways, but we must be willing to pay the cost of giving our life to Him—heart, will, mind and body—so that He has the freedom to do these things in us. The reality is that if Jesus is living His life in us, grace will have its way and we will see our lives transformed. From the day we are saved, His grace is building us up, training us, restoring, strengthening, and establishing us unto holiness. As we make room for this grace in our lives by dying to ourselves, the life of Jesus is manifested in us, which is the glory of God.

"For God, who said, 'Let light shine out of darkness,' has shone in our hearts to give the light of the knowledge of **the glory of God** in the face of Jesus Christ. But we have this treasure in jars of clay, to show that the surpassing **power belongs to God and not to us. For we who live are always being given over to death for Jesus' sake, so that the life of Jesus also may be manifested in our mortal flesh**" (2 Corinthians 4:6, 7, 11).

It is the unmerited favor of God's grace that He gives us what we need to live the sanctified life He has called us to. We are called to be holy and blameless before Him, even as in His grace, God has blessed us with every spiritual blessing in heavenly places that we need to glorify Him. He has given us everything we need that pertains to life and godliness. God does not ask us to glorify Him from ourselves based on the law, but He provides the grace for us as we pursue a relationship with Him and we seek to know who He is, so that His glory is revealed.

"Blessed be the God and Father of our Lord Jesus Christ, who has **blessed us in Christ with every spiritual blessing in the heavenly places,** even as he chose us in him before the foundation of the world, **that we should be holy and blameless before him**" (Ephesians 1:3-4).

"**His divine power has granted to us all things that pertain to life and godliness**, through the knowledge of him who called us to his own glory and excellence" (2 Peter 1:3).

Grace and Glory for Good Works

"But **by the grace of God** I am what I am, and his grace toward me was not in vain. On the contrary, **I worked harder than any of them, though it was not I, but the grace of God that is with me**" (1 Corinthians 15:10).

"And **God is able to make all grace abound to you**, so that having all sufficiency in all things at all times, **you may abound in every good work**" (2 Corinthians 9:8).

"**For by grace you have been** saved through faith. And this is not your own doing; it is the gift of God, not a result of works, so that no one may boast. For we are his workmanship, **created in Christ Jesus for good works, which God prepared beforehand, that we should walk in them**" (Ephesians 2:8-10).

"**For the grace of God** has appeared, bringing salvation for all people, training us to renounce ungodliness and worldly passions, and to live self-controlled, upright, and godly lives in the present age, waiting for our blessed hope, the appearing of the glory of our great God and Savior Jesus Christ, who gave himself for us to redeem us from all lawlessness and **to purify for himself a people for his own possession who are zealous for good works**" (Titus 2:11-14).

Often grace is understood to be the opposite of the law and works, and there are verses to support this view. However, to think of grace only as the antithesis of law and works is to neglect the full gospel that declares the grace of God to be working in our sanctification, as we have just seen, as well as the grace of God to do good works and to be empowered by the Holy Spirit. We do not earn grace leading to salvation by doing good works, but grace is the power for us to respond in love to the goodness, loving-kindness, and favor of God that saves and sanctifies us. It is the power of God to work in and through our lives to accomplish the good works He prepared for us to do beforehand in order to fulfill our calling. According to Titus 2, the ultimate purpose of the grace of God through salvation and the transformation of a sanctified life is to prepare a people "who are zealous for good works." Good works themselves are the grace of God that is in us, as Paul reveals in 1 Corinthians 15:10. With God, there is unlimited grace to do good works so that it can never be used as an excuse why good works aren't happening. According to Ephesians 2:10, we were created for good works which He prepared beforehand (before the foundations of the world) for us to do.

When the grace of God for us to do good works manifests, we will walk out our destiny and calling, which brings glory to God. That's how God foreordained it. How awesome that we are called and chosen by God to be in a relationship with Him, to be set apart for Him unto holiness, and to fulfill the purpose and destiny that He created us for. God chose you for two purposes. God created you to be in a love relationship with Him, where you are called to be the object of God's love and mercy and grace based on your position in Christ Jesus. Secondly, you have been chosen by His grace to bring the love you have received from God to other people. His love and grace are manifest through you in the good works that He has prepared for you to do. This will fulfill your destiny, which will glorify God, and will bring you to eternal glory. Oh, the grace of God to extend such glory to us! Oh, the glory of God to be so gracious to us!

> "The God of all **grace**, who has called you to his eternal **glory** in Christ" (1 Peter 5:10).

> "To this end we always pray for you, that our God may make you worthy of **his calling and may fulfill every resolve for good and every work of faith by his power**, so that the name of our Lord Jesus may be **glorified in you, and you in him, according to the grace** of our God and the Lord Jesus Christ" (2 Thessalonians 1:11-12).

By His grace, God glorifies Himself in us by calling us and giving us a purpose and destiny to glorify Him, even as He provides us with the power of His grace to do the good works which He has prepared for us to do, so that He is glorified in us and we are glorified in Him. The aim is that God's power and grace will produce good works according to our calling so that the name of Jesus is glorified in us. Because it is all of His grace, He gets all the glory!

Grace and Glory of Power

"*Charismata*" translated "gifts" is defined as extraordinary gifts of the Spirit bestowed upon Christians to equip them for the service of the church. The root word "*charis*" is "grace" "charismata" is really "gifts of grace." It is by the grace of God that we are empowered by the Holy Spirit to manifest His glory in gifts of service. We each may have different gifts, but they are all empowered by the same Spirit by the grace and strength that God supplies for the purpose that God would be glorified. It is the grace of God in Christ Jesus that makes all the gifts possible.

> "Having **gifts that differ according to the grace given to us**, let us use them: if prophecy\, in proportion to our faith; if service, in our serving; the one who teaches, in his teaching; the one who exhorts, in his exhortation; the one who contributes, in generosity; the one who leads, with zeal; the one who does acts of mercy, with cheerfulness" (Romans 12:6-8).

> "**As each has received a gift, use it to serve one another, as good stewards of God's varied grace**: whoever speaks, as one who speaks oracles of God; whoever serves, as one who serves by the strength

that God supplies—in order that in everything **God may be glorified through Jesus Christ.** To him belong glory and dominion forever and ever. Amen" (1 Peter 4:10-11).

"Now there are varieties of gifts, [charismata] but **the same Spirit**; and there are varieties of service, but the **same Lord**; and there are varieties of activities, but it is the **same God who empowers them all in everyone**. To each is given the manifestation of the Spirit for the common good" (1 Corinthians 11:4-7).

Since Pentecost, the grace of God is seen in power manifested by the Holy Spirit in us as believers. Every answered prayer, every work of service, every teaching or prophesy, every sign and wonder, every miraculous healing, is the grace of God found in Jesus Christ brought to us by the Holy Spirit for the glory of God! According to the gift of God's grace, He wants to work His power in and through each of our lives to manifest His glory to the world.

"And with **great power** the apostles were giving their testimony to the resurrection of the Lord Jesus, and **great grace** was upon them all" (Acts 4:33).

"And Stephen, **full of grace and power**, was **doing great wonders and signs** among the people" (Acts 6:8).

"Of this gospel I was made a minister according to the **gift of God's grace, which was given me by the working of his power**" (Ephesians 3:7).

Grace and Glory for Suffering

"But we see him who for a little while was made lower than the angels, namely **Jesus, crowned with glory and honor because of the suffering of death, so that by the grace of God he might taste death for everyone**" (Hebrews 2:9).

Not only is God's grace seen in the power of the Holy Spirit to see the supernatural victory of the cross, but God's grace and glory are also there in times of death, suffering, and delayed answer to prayer. Jesus' life and death prove this to us. Even though Jesus was fully God, He humbled Himself, became flesh, and dwelt among us. Jesus did not demand equality to God the Father but emptied

Himself and became nothing, taking the form of a human man. The fact that Jesus set aside His deity, took on the form of a human to submit Himself even to death on a cross as a criminal to die in our place, is His glory. Jesus' crucifixion is the reason that He is given the name that is above every name and that at the name of Jesus, every knee will bow and every tongue will confess that Jesus is God, which will also be to the glory of God the Father.

> "Christ Jesus, who, though he was in the form of God, did not count equality with God a thing to be grasped, but emptied himself, by taking the form of a servant, being born in the likeness of men. And being found in human form, **he humbled himself by becoming obedient to the point of death, even death on a cross. Therefore, God has highly exalted him and bestowed on him the name that is above every name**, so that at the name of Jesus every knee should bow, in heaven and on earth and under the earth, and every tongue confess that Jesus Christ is Lord, to the glory of God the Father" (Philippians 2:5-11).

Two times during the week before Jesus' death on the cross, He referred to His death as His "glorification." Jesus went to the cross with the purpose of glorifying the Father's name. He explained that it is like a seed, which is without glory until it dies in the ground and then grows into a plant bearing much fruit. Likewise, He had to die to bring forth good fruit that would glorify the Father, which would ultimately bring about His glory.

> "The hour has come for the Son of Man to be **glorified**. Truly, truly, I say to you, unless a grain of wheat falls into the earth and dies, it remains alone; but if it dies, it bears much fruit. Whoever loves his life loses it, and whoever hates his life in this world will keep it for eternal life... "Now is my soul troubled. And what shall I say? 'Father, save me from this hour'? But for this purpose, I have come to this hour. Father, **glorify your name**." Then a voice came from heaven: "**I have glorified it, and I will glorify it again**" (John 12:23-28).

> "When Jesus had spoken these words, he lifted up his eyes to heaven, and said, "Father, the hour has come; **glorify your Son that the Son may glorify you**, since you have given him authority over all flesh, to give eternal life to all whom you have given him. And this is eternal life, that they know you the only true God, and Jesus Christ whom you have sent. I **glorified** you on earth, having accomplished the work that you gave me to do. And now, Father, **glorify** me in your own presence

with the **glory** that I had with you before the world existed" (John 17:1-5).

Even as Christ was glorified in His suffering and death, we, as followers of Christ, are called to do likewise so that we may share in His sufferings, becoming like Him in His death. By God's grace, it is possible for us to follow Him and share in His suffering in order to share in His glory. In the same passage speaking of the glorification of His crucifixion in John 12, Jesus calls us to follow Him and be with Him in suffering, which will result in honor. If we suffer with Christ, we will be glorified with Him.

"**Whoever loves his life loses it, and whoever hates his life in this world will keep it for eternal life**. If anyone serves me, he must follow me; and where I am, there will my servant be also. If anyone serves me, the Father will honor him" (John 12:24-25).

"The Spirit himself bears witness with our spirit that we are children of God, and if children, then heirs—heirs of God and fellow heirs with Christ, **provided we suffer with him in order that we may also be glorified with him**" (Romans 8:16-17).

The fact of the matter is that throughout history, followers of Jesus have not been exempted from pain and suffering. At times, some have even suffered because of their faith in Jesus. Followers of Jesus around the world today are being persecuted for their faith.

"I have said these things to you, that in me you may have peace. **In the world you will have tribulation.** But take heart; I have overcome the world" (John 16:33).

"Strengthening the souls of the disciples, encouraging them to continue in the faith, and saying that **through many tribulations we must enter the kingdom of God**" (Acts 14:22).

"**Indeed, all who desire to live a godly life in Christ Jesus will be persecuted**" (2 Timothy 4:12).

"Beloved, do not be surprised at the fiery trial when it comes upon you to test you, as though something strange were happening to you. But **rejoice insofar as you share Christ's sufferings, that you may also**

rejoice and be glad when his glory is revealed. If you are insulted for the name of Christ, you are blessed, because the Spirit of glory and of God rests upon you" (1 Peter 4:12-14).

The Bible says that everybody suffers (2 Timothy 4:12). This will be especially true as the end times get closer and closer to Jesus' return. Jesus' return will be preceded by years of persecution and tribulation. Followers of Christ will suffer but have three promises.

First, God is always with us, as He has promised never to leave us nor forsake us (see Hebrews 13:5).

"But now thus says the LORD, he who created you, O Jacob, he who formed you, O Israel: "Fear not, for I have redeemed you; I have called you by name, you are mine. **When you pass through the waters, I will be with you; and through the rivers, they shall not overwhelm you; when you walk through fire you shall not be burned, and the flame shall not consume you.** For I am the LORD your God, the Holy One of Israel, your Savior" (Isaiah 43:1-3).

Second, God always gives us grace to endure, His presence comforts us, and His word guides us through every trouble. We actually come to know Him better in times of despair when we relinquish our own strength and depend on His power to deliver us. And He will deliver us.

"Blessed be the God and Father of our Lord Jesus Christ, the Father of mercies and **God of all comfort, who comforts us in all our affliction,** so that we may be able to comfort those who are in any affliction, with the comfort with which we ourselves are comforted by God. For **as we share abundantly in Christ's sufferings, so through Christ we share abundantly in comfort too**" (2 Corinthians 1:3-5).

"Indeed, we felt that we had received the sentence of death. But that was to make us rely not on ourselves but on God who raises the dead. **He delivered us** from such a deadly peril, and **he will deliver us. On him we have set our hope that he will deliver us again**" (2 Corinthians 1:9-10).

"Fear not, for I am with you; be not dismayed, for I am your God; **I will strengthen you, I will help you, I will uphold you** with my righteous right hand" (Isaiah 41:10).

"When the righteous cry for help, **the LORD hears and delivers them out of all their troubles.** The LORD is **near to the brokenhearted** and saves the crushed in spirit. Many are the afflictions of the righteous, but the LORD delivers him out of them all" (Psalm 34:17-19).

He is "near to the brokenhearted" and promises to "deliver us out of all our troubles." God gives us grace for suffering, which is sufficient to get us through the suffering. By standing in God's grace, His undeserved favor, when we are at our weakest, God's grace is the power that gets us through. He is strong and His grace is powerful enough to take what is evil and make good things out of it. He promises to restore, confirm, strengthen, and establish us. In the midst of our suffering, we can hope in the eternal grace and glory of God.

"And we know that for those who love God **all things work together for good**, for those who are called according to his purpose" (Romans 8:28).

"But he said to me, '**My grace is sufficient for you, for my power is made perfect in weakness**.' Therefore, I will boast all the more gladly of my weaknesses, so that the power of Christ may rest upon me" (1 Corinthians 12:9).

"And after you have suffered a little while, **the God of all grace, who has called you to his eternal glory in Christ, will himself restore, confirm, strengthen, and establish you**" (1 Peter 5:10).

Third, in so far as we share in Christ's suffering; we are blessed and share in the glory of God. The hope of eternal glory is at times the only hope that gets us through the suffering. The sufferings of this present time can't even compare to the glory that is to come. Suffering that is suffering for Jesus' sake will actually be rewarded with eternal glory in heaven. We can endure suffering by looking not at the things on earth that are seen and temporary, but by looking at the unseen eternal things and focusing on the glory to come.

"Blessed are those who are persecuted for righteousness' sake, **for theirs is the kingdom of heaven**. Blessed are you when others revile you and persecute you and utter all kinds of evil against you falsely on my account. Rejoice and be glad, **for your reward is great in heaven**, for so they persecuted the prophets who were before you" (Matthew 5:11-12).

"For I consider that the sufferings of this present time are **not worth comparing with the glory that is to be revealed to us**" (Romans 8:18).

"For this light momentary affliction is preparing for us an **eternal weight of glory beyond all comparison,** as we look not to the things that are seen but to the things that are unseen. For the things that are seen are transient, but the things that are unseen are eternal" (2 Corinthians 4:17-18).

"In this you rejoice, though now for a little while, if necessary, you have been grieved by various trials, so that the tested genuineness of your faith—more precious than gold that perishes though it is tested by fire—**may be found to result in praise and glory and honor at the revelation of Jesus Christ**" (1 Peter 1:6-7).

"Beloved, do not be surprised at the fiery trial when it comes upon you to test you, as though something strange were happening to you. But rejoice **insofar as you share Christ's sufferings, that you may also rejoice and be glad when his glory is revealed.** If you are insulted for the name of Christ, you are blessed, because the Spirit of glory and of God rests upon you" (1 Peter 4:12-14).

The secret to enduring suffering is to look not at the things on earth but to look at Jesus, the author and perfecter of our faith. Jesus is our only peace, hope, and comfort in our times of suffering. It is when we focus on Him and see the love in His eyes for us that all fear is cast out (see 1 John 4:18). It is when we see "the immeasurable greatness of his power toward us who believe" (Ephesians 1:19) that our hearts can be at rest. So let us lift our eyes and set our minds on Christ, who is seated at the right hand of God, reigning in all power and authority (see Colossians 3:1.) He is in control when things feel out of control for us. Let us "fix our eyes on Jesus" (Hebrews 12:2) so that we do not grow weary or lose heart. Let us follow His example by entrusting ourselves to God the Father while continuing to do what is right.

"If then you have been raised with Christ, seek the things that are above, where Christ is, seated at the right hand of God. **Set your minds on things that are above, not on things that are on earth**" (Colossians 3:1-2).

"**Looking to Jesus**, the founder and perfecter of our faith, **who for the joy that was set before him endured the cross, despising the shame**, and is seated at the right hand of the throne of God. Consider him who endured from sinners such hostility against himself, so that you may not grow weary or fainthearted" (Hebrews 12:2-3).

"For to this you have been called, **because Christ also suffered for you, leaving you an example, so that you might follow in his steps.** He committed no sin, neither was deceit found in his mouth. When he was reviled, he did not revile in return; when he suffered, he did not threaten, but continued **entrusting himself to him who judges justly**" (1 Peter 2:21-23).

"Therefore, let those who suffer according to God's will **entrust their souls to a faithful Creator while doing good**" (1 Peter 4:19).

Hebrews 12 says that Jesus endured the cross because of "the joy that was set before him." The joy of the cross was that after the cross there was the resurrection from the dead, ascension into heaven, a reigning at the right hand of the Father, and the Second Coming, where Jesus will return to earth as the Christ and Lord, forever and ever—this is the hope of eternal glory. We likewise have a joy set before us to look forward to the appearing of the glory of our great God and Savior, Jesus Christ, our hope of glory!

Glory at the Second Coming of Christ

"For **the Son of Man is going to come with his angels in the glory of his Father**, and then he will repay each person according to what he has done" (Matthew 16:27).

"Then will appear in heaven the sign of the Son of Man, and then all the tribes of the earth will mourn, and they will see **the Son of Man coming on the clouds of heaven with power and great glory**" (Matthew 24:30).

"When **the Son of Man comes in his glory**, and all the angels with him, then he will sit on his glorious throne" (Matthew 25:31).

What does the Bible say about our glorification? We have a great hope! Jesus is going to return to earth on the clouds, surrounded by angels with power and glory. Those who have already died when Christ returns, though they died with a mortal, perishable, natural body, will be resurrected with an immortal, imperishable, spiritual, glorified body! There will be no more death; there will only be life, and they will have a glorious body like Jesus'.

"So is it with the resurrection of the dead. What is sown is perishable; what is raised is imperishable. It is sown in dishonor; it is **raised in glory**. It is sown in weakness; it is raised in power. It is sown a natural body; it is raised a spiritual body. If there is a natural body, there is also a spiritual body" (1 Corinthians 15:42-44).

"Behold! I tell you a mystery. We shall not all sleep, but we shall all be changed, in a moment, in the twinkling of an eye, at the last trumpet. For the trumpet will sound, and the dead will be raised imperishable, and we shall be changed. For this perishable body must put on the imperishable, and this mortal body must put on immortality. When the perishable puts on the imperishable, and the mortal puts on immortality, then shall come to pass the saying that is written: "Death is swallowed up in victory. O death, where is your victory? O death, where is your sting?" The sting of death is sin, and the power of sin is the law. But thanks be to God, who gives us the victory through our Lord Jesus Christ" (1 Corinthians 15:51-57).

"But our citizenship is in heaven, and from it we await a Savior, the Lord Jesus Christ, who will **transform our lowly body to be like his glorious body**, by the power that enables him even to subject all things to himself" (Philippians 3:20-21).

"When Christ who is your life appears, then **you also will appear with him in glory**" (Colossians 3:4).

"But we do not want you to be uninformed, brothers, about those who are asleep, that you may not grieve as others do who have no hope. For since we believe that Jesus died and rose again, even so, through Jesus, God will bring with him those who have fallen asleep. For this we declare to you by a word from the Lord, that we who are alive, who are left until the coming of the Lord, will not precede those who have fallen asleep. For the Lord himself will descend from heaven with a cry of command, with the voice of an archangel, and with the sound of the trumpet of God. And the dead in Christ will rise first" (1 Thessalonians 4:13-17).

For those of us who are alive at Jesus' return, which I believe is more likely for future generations reading this book after the tribulation (see Revelation 6-11); the Lord Jesus will descend from heaven with power and great glory, and will send out His angels with a loud trumpet call to gather the followers of Jesus from one end of the heavens to the other. They will be caught up to meet Jesus in the air and be given immortal, imperishable, spiritual, glorified bodies.

"<u>Immediately after the tribulation</u> of those days the sun will be darkened, and the moon will not give its light, and the stars will fall from heaven, and the powers of the heavens will be shaken. Then will appear in heaven the sign of the Son of Man, and then all the tribes of the earth will mourn, and they will see **the Son of Man coming on the clouds of heaven with power and great glory**. And he will send out his angels with a loud trumpet call, and they will gather his elect from the four winds, from one end of heaven to the other" (Matthew 24:29-31).

"Then we who are alive, who are left, will be caught up together with them in the clouds to meet the Lord in the air, and so we will always be with the Lord. Therefore, encourage one another with these words" (1 Thessalonians 4:18).

Eternal Glory

After the judgment, those whose names are written in the Book of Life will experience eternity with God. We will be His sons and daughters; He will be our God. He will wipe away every tear from our eyes; there will be no more death, nor mourning, nor crying, nor pain. For the former things will be passed away, and we will drink from the spring of living water forever!

"Then one of the elders addressed me, saying, 'Who are these, clothed in white robes, and from where have they come?' I said to him, 'Sir, you know.' And he said to me, 'These are the ones <u>coming out of the great tribulation</u>. They have washed their robes and made them white in the blood of the Lamb. Therefore, they are before the throne of God, and serve him day and night in his temple; and he who sits on the throne will shelter them with his presence. **They shall hunger no more, neither thirst anymore; the sun shall not strike them, nor any scorching heat. For the Lamb in the midst of the throne will be their shepherd, and he will guide them to springs of living water, and God will wipe away every tear from their eyes'"** (Revelation 7:13-17).

"Then I saw a new heaven and a new earth, for the first heaven and the first earth had passed away, and the sea was no more. And I saw the holy city, new Jerusalem, coming down out of heaven from God, prepared as a bride adorned for her husband. And I heard a loud voice from the throne saying, 'Behold, the dwelling place of God is with man. He will dwell with them, and they will be his people, and God himself will be with them as their God. **He will wipe away every tear from their eyes, and death shall be no more, neither shall there be mourning, nor crying, nor pain anymore, for the former things have passed away.'** And he who was seated on the throne said, 'Behold, I am making all things new.' Also, he said, 'Write this down, for these words are trustworthy and true.' And he said to me, 'It is done! I am the Alpha and the Omega, the beginning and the end. To the thirsty I will give from the spring of the water of life without payment. The one who conquers will have this heritage, and I will be his God and he will be my son'" (Revelation 21:1-7).

"Then the angel showed me the river of the water of life, bright as crystal, flowing from the throne of God and of the Lamb through the middle of the street of the city; also, on either side of the river, the tree of life with its twelve kinds of fruit, yielding its fruit each month. **The leaves of the tree were for the healing of the nations. No longer will there be anything accursed, but the throne of God and of the Lamb will be in it, and his servants will worship him**. They will see his face, and his name will be on their foreheads. And night will be no more. They will need no light of lamp or sun, for the Lord God will be their light, and they will reign forever and ever" (Revelation 22:1-5).

This is our great hope for eternity. We will be with God, we will finally be able to see His face, we will be like Him (see 1 John 3:2), and we will know Him even as we are known by Him (see 1 Corinthians 13:12). He will be our light and we will never again experience darkness. Finally, knowing and seeing Jesus Christ will be our great reward for He will be our delight and glory for eternity.

The Hope of the Glory of God

"Through him we have also obtained access by faith into this **grace** in which we stand, and we rejoice in **hope of the glory of God**" (Romans 5:2).

"Waiting for our **blessed hope, the appearing of the glory of our great God and Savior** Jesus Christ" (Titus 2:13).

"The God of all **grace**, who has **called you to his eternal glory in Christ**" (1 Peter 5:10).

Hope is a feeling of expectation; the feeling that what we want or desire is going to happen and will turn out for good in the end. Our hope is that we will share in the glory of Jesus Christ at His second coming. We will stand in God's grace, His unmerited favor to us, where we are called to eternal glory to be with Christ Jesus. First, Jesus will return with power and great glory; then He will sit on His glorious throne and reign throughout eternity as King of kings and Lord of lords, and we will reign with Him in glory forever.

Until Jesus comes, may you continually grow in the grace and knowledge of the mystery of Jesus Christ Who is living in you as your hope of glory. As you pursue Him, know that Jesus is able to make all grace abound toward you, for He is able, and He has all sufficiency to keep you from stumbling and present you blameless before God at His second coming. To Jesus Christ, be the glory now and for eternity!

"And **God is able to make all grace abound to you**, so that having all sufficiency in all things at all times, you may abound in every good work" (2 Corinthians 9:8).

"But **grow in the grace and knowledge of our Lord and Savior Jesus Christ**. To him be the **glory** both now and to the day of eternity. Amen" (2 Peter 3:18).

"Now to him who is able to keep you from stumbling and to present you blameless before the presence of his glory with great joy, to the only God, our Savior, through Jesus Christ our Lord, be glory, majesty, dominion, and authority, before all time and now and forever. Amen" (Jude 1:24-25).

CHAPTER 12 Questions for Thought and Discussion

1. The question is asked "What shall we say then? Are we to continue in sin that grace may abound?" (Romans 6:1) How would you answer this question? (See Romans 6:2-7 for the Bible's answer.)

2. In living the Christian life, what is God responsible for? What are you responsible for?

   "Therefore, my beloved, as you have always obeyed, so now, not only as in my presence but much more in my absence, work out your own salvation with fear and trembling, for it is God who works in you, both to will and to work for his good pleasure" **(Philippians 2:12-13).**

3. How does God's grace apply to sanctification, good works, and the gifts of power?

4. a) Which requires more grace: miracles and healings or enduring suffering?

   b) How is God's grace sufficient in times of suffering according to 1 Corinthians 12:9, "My grace is sufficient for you, for my power is made perfect in weakness"?

5. What are keys to growing in and being strengthened in grace?

6. a) What is the glory of God that we can enjoy now?

   b) What will be the glory we can look forward to in the future?

Appendix A
Assurance Verses

Assurance of Salvation	John 5:24	1 John 5:11-13
Assurance of New Life	2 Corinthians 5:17	Galatians 2:20
Assurance of Forgiveness	I John 1:8-9	Hebrews 8:12
Assurance of Right Standing	Romans 5:1	2 Corinthians 5:21
Assurance of Answered Prayer	John 16:24	Philippians 4:6-7
Assurance of God's Presence	Hebrews 13:5	Psalm 139:7-10
Assurance of God's Help	Isaiah 41:10	Matthew 11:28-30
Assurance of God's Peace	John 14:27	John 16:33
Assurance of God's Victory	1 Corinthians 10:13	Philippians 4:13
Assurance of God's Provision	Philippians 4:19	Matthew 6:31-33
Assurance of God's Protection	2 Thessalonians 3:3	Psalm 91
Assurance of God's Love	Romans 8:38-39	Psalm 103:7-13
Assurance of God's Acceptance	Romans 8:1	Hebrews 4:15-16
Assurance of Guidance	Proverbs 3:5-6	John 16:13
Assurance of Blessing	Ephesians 1:3	2 Peter 1:3
Assurance of Healing	Psalm 103:3	1 Peter 2:24
Assurance of God's voice	Jeremiah 33:3	John 10:27
Assurance of the Holy Spirit	Luke 11:9-13	John 14:16-18

Appendix B

Who I am in Christ

Used by permission. Victory Over the Darkness, by Neil Anderson, pp. 38-39.
Copyright (2000), Gospel Light/Regal Books, Ventura, CA 93003.
www.ficm.org/index.php?command=textwhoamiinchrist

I am accepted...
John 1:12	I am God's child.
John 15:15	As a disciple, I am a friend of Jesus Christ.
Romans 5:1	I have been justified.
1 Corinthians 6:17	I am united with the Lord, and I am one with Him in spirit.
1 Corinthians 6:19-20	I have been bought with a price and I belong to God.
1 Corinthians 1	I am a member of Christ's body.
Ephesians 1:3-8	I have been chosen by God and adopted as His child.
Colossians 1:13-14	I have been redeemed and forgiven of all my sins.
Colossians 2:9-10	I am complete in Christ.
Hebrews 4:14-16	I have direct access to the throne of grace through Jesus Christ.

I am secure...
Romans 8:1-2	I am free from condemnation.
Romans 8:28	I am assured that God works for my good in all circumstances.
Romans 8:31-39	I am free from any condemnation brought against me and I cannot be separated from the love of God.
2 Corinthians 1:21-22	I have been established, anointed and sealed by God.
Colossians 3:1-4	I am hidden with Christ in God.
Philippians 1:6	God will complete the good work He started in me.
Philippians 3:20	I am a citizen of heaven.
2 Timothy 1:7	I have not been given a spirit of fear but of power, love and a sound mind.
1 John 5:18	I am born of God and the evil one cannot touch me.

I am significant...
John 15:5	I am a branch of Jesus Christ, the true vine, a channel of His life.
John 15:16	I have been chosen and appointed to bear fruit.
1 Corinthians 3:16	I am God's temple.
2 Corinthians 5:17-21	I am a minister of reconciliation for God.
Ephesians 2:6	I am seated with Jesus Christ in the heavenly realm.
Ephesians 2:10	I am God's workmanship.
Ephesians 3:12	I may approach God with freedom and confidence.
Philippians 4:13	I can do all things through Christ, who strengthens me.

Appendix C
Who is Jesus: Study of the Gospel of John

One of my favorite Bible studies is to study the Book of John asking three questions.

"Who does Jesus say that He is?"
"Why did He say He came?"
"What does He say that He wants from me?"

When making a list of "who Jesus says He is," we find that Jesus said over and over again "I am..." Jesus said "I am the: Word, Light, Life, Way, Truth, Bread, Good Shepherd, Door, Vine, Bridegroom, Farmer, just to name a few. Each of these pictures is a theme that is discussed more than once in John and other places in Scripture. Each of these comes with a story Jesus told to explain how He is like all of these things. Jesus was trying to make Himself and God the Father known in terms that were understandable to regular people. He used the simple things in life to illustrate who He is and what He is like. Jesus is clearly longing for us to know Him so that we call on His name and grow in relationship with Him.

Suggested study: As you read through the Gospel of John, make three lists of the verses that answer the above questions and jot down a note about what Jesus is saying in each verse.

List 1) Jesus says, "I am the ..."

List 2) Jesus says "I have come that..."

List 3) Jesus says He wants me to....

Appendix D

How to Make Jesus Savior and Lord

"Let all the house of Israel therefore know for certain that God has made him both Lord and Christ, this Jesus whom you crucified." Now when they heard this they were cut to the heart, and said to Peter and the rest of the apostles, "Brothers, what shall we do?" And Peter said to them, "**Repent and be baptized every one of you in the name of Jesus Christ for the forgiveness of your sin**" (Acts 2:36-39).

When Peter finished preaching, the people were convinced that Jesus was indeed the Lord and Christ they had been waiting for. They were cut to the heart and asked what they should do. Peter answered that they needed to "repent." "Repent" means to feel and confess sincere regret or remorse about wrongdoing or sin and make a decision to go the other direction. It literally means to "turn" or "return," or to "change your mind or purpose." In this case, it means to turn from our sin and going our own way to going God's way. When we repent before God in prayer, our sins are forgiven. We are forgiven by bringing our sins to Jesus so that the punishment He endured on the cross that we deserved, would pay our debt and we can be completely acquitted for all our sins and our sinful condition. In the place of sin, Jesus gives us new life in Himself.

> "Thus, it is written, that the Christ should suffer and on the third day rise from the dead, and that **repentance and forgiveness of sins should be proclaimed in his name** to all nations" (Luke 24:46-47).

> "**Repent therefore, and turn again, that your sins may be blotted out**, that times of refreshing may come from the presence of the Lord, and that he may send the Christ appointed for you, Jesus" (Acts 3:19).

There are a few facets to the process of repenting and making Jesus your Savior and Lord. Some of these happen at once, in a split second. Some may take time for you to process in your heart but culminate in a change of heart expressed in a prayer to Jesus that only takes a few seconds. Let's look at the four facets of repenting and putting your faith in Jesus Christ as your Savior and Lord that we each must engage in.

<u>Confess Sin</u>

Admit that you are a sinner and that you have been going your own way. Admit any specific sins God has brought to mind and those you have been feeling guilty about. Admit that you sin all the time so that you can't possibly name every sin. Going your own way involves good things that are not necessarily bad but may not be what God wants for you. Since the foundation of the world, God has a good plan and purpose for your life! You must turn from going your own way and be willing to go God's way, knowing that He loves us and has good planned for you. Ask God to help you be willing to make that change.

> "**For all have sinned** and fall short of the glory of God" (Romans 3:23).

> "The fool says in his heart, "There is no God." They are corrupt, doing abominable iniquity; there is none who does good. God looks down from heaven on the children of man to see if there are any who understand, who seek after God. **They have all fallen away; together they have become corrupt; there is none who does good, not even one**" (Psalm 53:1-3).

> "If we say we have no sin, we deceive ourselves, and the truth is not in us. **If we confess our sins, he is faithful and just to forgive us our sins and to cleanse us from all unrighteousness**" (1 John 1:8-9).

> "**All we like sheep have gone astray; we have turned—every one—to his own way;** and the LORD has laid on him the iniquity of us all" (Isaiah 53:6).

Have Godly Sorrow

Have Godly sorrow or remorse for your sin. If you are truly repentant for your sin and going your own way, you will feel sorry for grieving God as you have sinned against Him and have contributed to Jesus' suffering on the cross. Often you will feel remorse for sinning and going your own way because it has cost you dearly as you have hurt yourself and other people.

> "For **godly grief produces a repentance** that leads to salvation without regret, whereas worldly grief produces death" (2 Corinthians 7:10).

Ask to Be Forgiven

Ask Jesus to take the punishment for your sin so you don't have to. Acknowledge that you are helpless to help yourself but that you are putting all your hope in Jesus, who took your punishment by dying on the cross in your place. Identify with Jesus on the cross by desiring to be dead to your sin and alive to a resurrected new life in Jesus.

"And you, who were dead in your trespasses and the uncircumcision of your flesh, God made alive together with him, **having forgiven us all our trespasses, by canceling the record of debt that stood against us with its legal demands. This he set aside, nailing it to the cross**" (Colossians 2:13-14).

Invite Jesus into Your Heart

Invite Jesus into your life as Savior and Lord. As Savior, you are giving Him your sins and asking Him to take them to the cross and forgive you. In place of your sins, Jesus will give you, His righteousness. As Lord, it means you are no longer in control, He is and you are giving Him your life to lead! In place of going your own way, you must tell God you will make a decision of your will to go His way. Won't you invite Jesus's Holy Spirit into your heart now to be with you, to change your life, and to fellowship with you?

"Behold, I stand at the door and knock. If anyone hears my voice and opens the door, **I will come in to him and eat with him, and he with me" (Revelation 3:20).**

Sample Prayer:

Heavenly Father, I confess that my entire life I have been living in sin and going my own way. I am deeply sorry for sinning against You in all these ways. I admit that I am helpless to save myself and that my only hope is in Jesus' death on the cross in my place for the forgiveness of my sins. Please forgive my sin and count Jesus' punishment in my place. I invite You, Jesus, into my life as my Savior and Lord. Please fill me with Your Holy Spirit. I will follow You forever and turn from going my own way. Thank You for saving me from death and giving me new life in Jesus Christ. Amen.

Praise God! The Bible says that your decision to follow Jesus causes great rejoicing in heaven! God is full of joy to have His relationship with you restored! He is happy to have His child back!

"Just so, I tell you, there will be more joy in heaven over one sinner who repents than over ninety-nine righteous persons who need no repentance" (Luke 15:7).

This is the greatest decision you have ever made. Your life will never be the same. By accepting Jesus as your Savior and Lord, you are forgiven which means you will not only have eternal life with God after you die, but eternal life starts right now, the minute you give your life to Jesus. Jesus has redeemed your life from the pain, suffering, sickness, and problems sin has caused here on the earth. More than that, you have been justified so that He no longer sees your sins, but only sees you robed in the righteousness of Jesus. Your relationship with God as a son or daughter has been reconciled once and for all!

Forgiveness and salvation are the greatest gifts of God, but they are only just the beginning, just the entrance into all the awesome things God has for you. Once you accepted the forgiveness of your sins and invited Christ into your life, your old life was nailed to the cross and died with Jesus and He has given you a new life. Your old life is gone and you have a new life, Christ living His life in you. Now everything is made new, beautiful, and alive!

> "Therefore, **if anyone is in Christ, he is a new creation. The old has passed away; behold, the new has come**" (2 Corinthians 5:17).

> "**I have been crucified with Christ. It is no longer I who live, but Christ who lives in me**. And the life I now live in the flesh I live by faith in the Son of God, who loved me and gave himself for me" (Galatians 2:20).

After Jesus is Your Savior and Lord

1. Be assured that God has forgiven you.

If you have confessed your sin, the Bible says that you are forgiven and that God remembers your sins no more.

> "If we confess our sins, he is faithful and just to forgive us our sins and to cleanse us from all unrighteousness" (1 John 1:8-9).

> "As far as the east is from the west, so far does he remove our transgressions from us" (Psalm 103:12).

> "Come now, let us reason together, says the LORD: though your sins are like scarlet, they shall be as white as snow; though they are red like crimson, they shall become like wool" (Isaiah 1:18).

> "I, I am he who blots out your transgressions for my own sake, and I will not remember your sins" (Isaiah 43:25).

> "He will again have compassion on us; he will tread our iniquities underfoot. You will cast all our sins into the depths of the sea" (Micah 7:19).

2. Be assured of your salvation.

If you have invited Jesus into your life, you are saved because "He who has the Son has life!" God wants you to <u>know</u> that you have eternal life. Believe it, it's true!

> "But to all who did receive him, who believed in his name, he gave the right to become children of God" (John 1:12).

> "Truly, truly, I say to you, whoever hears my word and believes him who sent me has eternal life. He does not come into judgment, but has passed from death to life" (John 5:24).

> "God gave us eternal life, and this life is in his Son. Whoever has the Son has life; whoever does not have the Son of God does not have life. I write these things to you who believe in the name of the Son of God **that you may know** that you have eternal life" (1 John 5:10-13).

3. Confess out loud.

Confess out loud that Jesus is your Savior and Lord. Tell somebody about the decision you have made. Find other Christians to fellowship with and tell them about your new decision to follow Christ Jesus.

> "If you confess with your mouth that Jesus is Lord and believe in your heart that God raised him from the dead, you will be saved. For with the heart, one believes and is justified, and with the mouth one confesses and is saved. For the Scripture says, "Everyone who believes in him will not be put to shame ... For everyone who calls on the name of the Lord will be saved" (Romans 10:9-10).

4. Change Directions.

Having made Jesus Lord by declaring that you are willing to give up going your own way, now begin going Jesus' way and obeying Him with every little decision in life. Confess any sin that God brings to mind, turn and begin going God's direction. Obey the Holy Spirit's prompting as you make the necessary changes in your life and circumstances to come into obedience to Christ. Cooperate with God as He works in your life to change you and to give you new life through His Spirit living in you.

> "If you love me, you will keep my commandments ...Whoever has my commandments and keeps them, he it is who loves me. And he who loves me will be loved by my Father, and I will love him and manifest myself to him" (John 14:15, 21).

> "Let not sin therefore reign in your mortal body, to make you obey its passions. Do not present your members to sin as instruments for

unrighteousness, but present yourselves to God as those who have been brought from death to life, and your members to God as instruments for righteousness" (Romans 6:12-13).

"And he [*Jesus*] said to all, "If anyone would come after me, let him deny himself and take up his cross daily and follow me. For whoever would save his life will lose it, but whoever loses his life for my sake will save it. For what does it profit a man if he gains the whole world and loses or forfeits himself?" (Luke 9:23-25)

This new life with God is so awesome; no one would ever want his or her old life back!!! Therefore, it is easy to give up your old life, to give up going your own way, and to begin going God's way. God's way is life and peace and joy! His commands are not burdensome! They become a joy to follow because we know they are a blessing for our good. We are glad to be able to glorify God with our life in response to all the great awesome things He has done for us!

"For this is the love of God, that we keep his commandments. And his commandments are not burdensome" (1 John 5:3).

"This God--his way is perfect; the word of the LORD proves true; he is a shield for all those who take refuge in him" (Psalm 18:30).

"Your way, O God, is holy. What god is great like our God?" (Psalm 77:13).

"Blessed are those whose way is blameless, who walk in the law of the LORD! Blessed are those who keep his testimonies, who seek him with their whole heart, who also do no wrong, but walk in his ways!" (Psalm 119:1-3).

Since God loved you so much to send Jesus to die for you, there is no limit to the love that He will lavish on you and the good things He promises to give you. He is able to give you abundantly more than you could even think to ask for! He promises you an abundant life in Him.

"What then shall we say to these things? If God is for us, who can be against us? He who did not spare his own Son but gave him up for us all, how will he not also with him graciously give us all things?" (Rom 8:31-32).

"Now to him who is able to do far more abundantly than all that we ask or think, according to the power at work within us" (Ephesians 3:20).

"I came that they may have life and have it abundantly" (John 10:10).

There is so much to learn and experience in going God's way that it will take your whole life to understand, receive, apply and grow into the full potential that God has in store for you. And this is just the beginning; in eternity, He offers us so much more that our minds can't even comprehend it now!

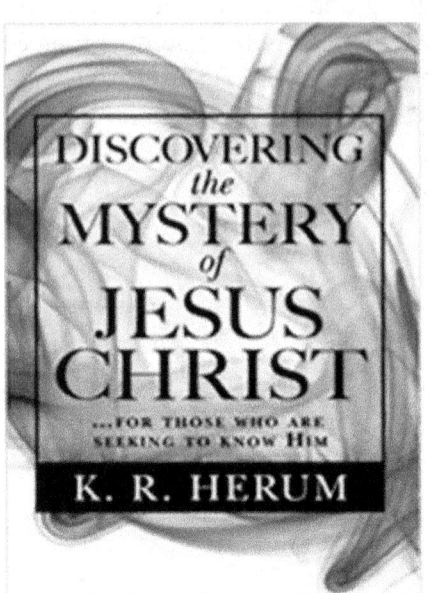 

Discovering the Mystery of Jesus Christ (2013) is for those who are truly seeking to find God. Would you like to satisfy the longing of your heart? Do you want to find meaning for your life? Would you like a relationship with God for now and eternity? *Discovering the Mystery of Jesus Christ* is passionately written to clearly and logically begin to explain how God made it possible through Jesus Christ for each of us to have a personal relationship with Him and the many awesome blessings that come with being in relationship with Jesus.

Discovering the Revelation of Jesus Christ (2024) is a chronological study of the book of Revelation which reveals God's end time plan. It is supported and interpreted by Old Testament prophesy from 150 chapters of the Bible, explaining the timing, imagery, and symbols by using Scripture to interpret itself. This study covers the history of the world, beginning with the writing of Revelation by the Apostle John, until Jesus' return, and into eternity. It interprets the Letters to the Seven Churches, the Seven Seals, and the Seven Trumpets in the context of world history and end time geopolitical events. It introduces and identifies the main end time characters: the Two Prophets, the Beast, the Antichrist, the False Prophet, the Harlot, and Mystery Babylon. It brings understanding to the Millennium, the millennial temple, the New Heavens and New Earth, and the New Jerusalem. *Discovering the Revelation of Jesus Christ* reveals that end time prophesy has been fulfilled in history and continues to be fulfilled by current geopolitics. The historical and geopolitical research supporting the spiritual emphasis of this book is provided by the same author in *The Fourth Beast of the New World Order* and *The Four Horsemen of the New World Order*.

This is My Blood (2015) Experience intimacy with Jesus by studying the ten blessings the Bible specifically attributes to Jesus' shed blood on the cross. Understanding the blood of Jesus will enable you to experience intimacy with God and enjoy all the benefits that Jesus provided for you in His death on the cross.

This is My Body (2015) examines the different aspects in which Jesus died to His flesh and applies it to what it means for us to die to our flesh to share in His suffering. By denying ourself, we can experience the sanctification of our soul, intimacy with God, and empowering of the Holy Spirit we long for.

**Books can be purchased on Amazon.com or on Ebay.com
Or the author can be contacted by email at** krherum@gmail.com

The Fourth Beast of the New World Order (2023)
is based on the revelation that the Fourth Beast of Daniel 7 and Revelation 13 is the geo-political system that is creating the New World Order today. The global elite have secretly created a vast strategic network, whose current goal is to cull the population and destroy western civilization, in order to establish the New World Order. Cloaking the world in Babylonian paganism to accomplish their goal, they are creating a One World government and One World religion as necessary preparation for the coming of the Antichrist. *The Fourth Beast of the New World Order* gives a broad overview of history and current events; putting all the pieces together to gain a logical outline of the of the New World Order. This book answers the question of who the global elite are, what they are doing and why, and how they are fulfilling Bible prophecy.

The Four Horsemen of the New World Order (2024)
interprets the Four Seals of Revelation 6 in the context of the New World Order. It will study various topics in history and current events over the past 2000 years to show how they fit into the end times prophesied in Scripture. The Four Horsemen will be interpreted as the White Horse – Catholicism, the Red Horse – Communism, the Black Horse – Capitalism, and the Green Horse – Technocracy. The book gives a deep detailed look at who these Four Horsemen are and how they are active in the world today working to create the Global World Government and One World Religion as necessary preparation for the coming of the Antichrist. *The Four Horsemen of the New World Order* is an in-depth study that is the companion book to *The Fourth Beast of the New World Order* which gives an introductory overview of the elite attempting to build the New World Order. Both books stand on their own.

Books can be purchased on Amazon.com or on Ebay.com
Or the author can be contacted by email at krherum@gmail.com

www.ingramcontent.com/pod-product-compliance
Lightning Source LLC
LaVergne TN
LVHW051827080426
835512LV00018B/2765